FOREST

of

OKLAHOMA

How To Know Them

A POCKET MANUAL

by

WILBUR R. MATTOON,
Extension Forester, Forest Service,
U. S. Department of Agriculture,
Washington, D. C.

and

GEORGE R. PHILLIPS,
State Forester of Oklahoma,
State Capitol, Oklahoma City,
Oklahoma.

FOREWORD

This handbook has been prepared in response to a growing demand for information regarding our common forest trees. These requests are largely the result of a widening appreciation of the possibilities of tree planting as a means of producing a marketable commodity of increasing value that will add yearly to the farm income as well as enhance the value of the farm, both as a salable property and as a comfortable and attractive home.

Oklahoma has many trees producing useful and valuable wood and others that may be successfully planted. Timber is the best crop to grow on certain soils and locations on the farm. Many farmers have, for example, some hillsides or wornout gullied sandy or wet lands better adapted for growing timber than any other crop. To rightly utilize all the farm is a sign of good farm management.

It is natural for young people to be interested in trees. Many will become farm owners of the future, and a knowledge of trees will add an interest in their lives and prove to be a very material asset. School teachers, county agents, scout leaders, etc., who deal with both present and future owners of timberland, will be aided by this manual in acquiring a better knowledge of the uses and value of our forest trees.

Altogether 74 trees are described, with a brief description or mention of 35 other varieties or species, all of which are native or very extensively planted in the State.

Grateful acknowledgement is hereby made to the State Forestry Departments of Maryland, Virginia, North Carolina and Tennessee and to the Botanical Departments of the Colleges of Agriculture of Arkansas and Mississippi for the use of portions of the text. All of the cuts of the hardwoods are from original drawings by Mrs. E. A. Hoyle, of the United States Forest Service, while those of the five conifers are from Sargent's "Manual of the Trees of North America," by permission of Houghton-Mifflin Company.

The rapidly increasing interest in outdoor life, stimulated by good roads, the automobile, the boy's and girl's club and scout movements, and the widened outlook resulting from the spread of education, encourages the rational treatment of our trees and forests. It is highly important that this be done in order that our forests may continue to furnish the material so essential to the maintenance of the industrial and social life of the State and Nation, to protect our farmsteads and mountain streams, and to provide places of pleasure and recreation for our people.

THE OKLAHOMA FOREST COMMISSION

MEMBERS

Mr. Harry B. Cordell, President, State Board of Agriculture, Oklahoma City, Oklahoma, Chairman.

Mrs. I. L. Huff, Sapulpa, Vice-chairman.

Dr. Bradford A. Knapp, President, Oklahoma A. and M. College, Stillwater.

Mr. John F. Easley, Ardmore.

Mr. John M. Craig, Idabel.

SECRETARY AND STATE FORESTER

George R. Phillips, State Capitol, Oklahoma City, Oklahoma.

The Oklahoma Forest Commission is composed of the President of the State Board of Agriculture, who is ex-officio chairman; the President of the Oklahoma A. and M. College; a representative of the State Federation of Women's Clubs, appointed by the Governor from a list of five names submitted to him by the Executive Board of the Federation of Clubs; and two members appointed by the Governor.

The Commission employs a technically trained forester to act as its Secretary and State Forester.

Headquarters of the Commission are in the offices of the State Board of Agriculture at the State Capitol, Oklahoma City, Oklahoma.

The efforts of the Forest Commission have been directed along several lines of endeavor. In cooperation with the U. S. Forest Service and private land owners, fire protection has been established on 1,312,000 acres in southeastern Oklahoma. By this means and by exercise of proper cutting methods it is hoped to keep this portion of the State forever producing a profitable crop of trees.

In cooperation with the U. S. Forest Service a forest nursery has been established on the grounds of the A. and M. College at Stillwater on land donated by the College. It is planned to grow in and distribute from this nursery forest planting stock suitable for woodlot and windbreak planting on the farms of the State. Trees will be available only for the above purposes and will be sold at a nominal price.

An educational campaign encouraging the planting of trees about homes, public buildings, school houses, along highways, and for woodlot and windbreak purposes is being conducted. It is in connection with this work and with the idea of making Oklahomans generally acquainted with the forests and trees we already have that publication of this booklet was made possible.

WHAT IS FORESTRY?

Forestry, in brief, may be defined as the art and science of forming, caring for or cultivating forests.

Were it defined as applied to the great State of Oklahoma as a whole it would necessitate a much more elaborate and involved definition than this.

Proper application of forestry principles in management of woodlands for profitable production of forest products may be likened to a bank and its operation. The ground upon which forests grow may be compared to the building in which the banking institution is housed. The growing stock, or forest growth on the land, represents money deposited in the bank as a savings account. The larger the savings account, hence the larger the growing stock of trees, the greater will be the returns.

The savings account or growing stock is deposited for the return, the interest, which it will accumulate. The annual growth or increment of the trees is the interest. This may be cut off each year in the form of posts, poles, fuel and lumber without in any way diminishing the capital stock or savings account.

Certain factors favorable to proper management of the land and growing stock so that a maximum return may be netted are proper cutting policies, careful logging methods, removal of undesirable trees and species from the stand, and protected from fire. Elimination of livestock grazing, particularly in hardwood forests, is an equally important factor. It is the practical application of these and other factors to increase forest land yields which make up applied forestry.

Planting of trees in the form of windbreaks and farm woodlands, for the protection of buildings, livestock and orchards and for the forest products such as posts, poles, fuel and lumber they will produce is equally a form of applied forestry. These artificial forests often play additional important roles such as preventing soil from eroding and holding stream banks from caving in.

FOREST CONDITIONS IN OKLAHOMA

Oklahoma, a great area of 44,424,960 acres, with her southern corner only about 400 feet and her northwestern corner nearly 5,000 feet above sea level, with an annual precipitation of 45 inches in her southeastern section dwindling to but little over 15 inches in her northwestern portion, presents a wonderfully varied set of conditions to those interested in her forests and in tree planting.

The native forests range from the bottomland hardwoods and shortleaf pine---oak types of the extreme southeast, through the hardwood type of the Ozarks, the black-jack oak---post oak type, on through the prairies where the only native trees occur along streams and in canyons, to the foothill type of the Rockies where pinon pine and scrubby oaks form the major portion of the ground cover.

Originally Oklahoma had about 12,000,000 acres, or 27 percent of her total area, covered with forests. Today approximately 8,000,000 acres, or 18 percent of her area, are still covered with tree growth. The shortleaf pine-oak type, the most important commercial type, covers about 2,500,000 acres, the other 5,500,-000 acres being popularly known as black-jack oak-post oak land.

Oklahoma has need of all the trees she now possesses and of many others in addition. Practically all of the present forested area is so rough, topographically, and has such infertile soil that it will be impossible of cultivation for annual crops or will, at best, be sub-marginal from an agricultural standpoint. This means that it should always be kept at work producing the only crop it is capable of growing---trees. Protection from forest fires is an absolute essential if this is to be carried out.

Forests can be made to perpetuate themselves only if the young trees are allowed to grow up and replace the old ones that die or are cut for commercial purposes. Fires kill these little trees and damage the older ones.

Rough, hilly land can best be kept from eroding if covered with forest growth. The roots in the ground and the leaves, twigs, and humus on top of the ground hold the soil in place. Fire destroys this mulch, allow-

5

ing stormwaters to rush off rapidly and wash away the soil.

Trees and shrubs in the forest form protective cover and their fruits form a source of food supply for game animals and birds. Fires destroy these little trees and shrubs with their attendant benefits, thus forcing the game out of the country.

A practical cutting plan should be followed to keep the forests at their highest possible production point. Already our largest lumber company has adopted a policy whereby pines below a diameter of twelve inches are not cut, thus assuring an adequate growing stock on the ground at all times. Owners of smaller blocks of forest---farmers and lumbermen---should fall in line with this or a similar plan.

Western Oklahoma, where little natural tree growth occurs, particularly needs trees. Windbreaks about buildings, feeding lots and orchards should be established. Belts of trees along fields for protection from hot winds should be planted. Woodlots on waste land and on land liable to erode, especially along stream banks, would provide post and fuel supplies and prevent much loss of fertile surface soil. Shade trees planted about homes, public buildings, school houses and along highways would all help to make the region more attractive and comfortable.

Trees will grow in western Oklahoma. Widely scattered plantings, mostly of black locust and Russian mulberry, testify to this fact to varying degrees. Of especial value are the plantings on the grounds of the Woodward Field Station of the U. S. Bureau of Plant Industry where over a period of thirteen years many species of shrubs and trees have been planted. Of particular interest because of successful growth are Scotch pine, western yellow pine and Chinese arbor vitae among the evergreens, and Chinese elm, American elm, honey locust, sycamore, silver maple, Russian olive, cottonwood, osage orange, hackberry and green ash among the deciduous species.

SHORTLEAF PINE (Yellow Pine)
(*Pinus echinata* Mill.)

The shortleaf pine, also known as yellow or rosemary pine, is widely distributed throughout the eastern part of the state. It is the common pine of the hills and in the lowlands it forms pure stands. The young

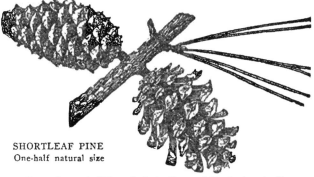

SHORTLEAF PINE
One-half natural size

From Sargent's "Manual of the Trees of North America,"
by permission of Houghton-Mifflin Company

tree has a straight and stout stem with slightly ascending branches. The mature tree has a tall, straight stem and an oval crown, reaching a height of about 100 feet and a diameter of about 4½ feet. The young tree, when cut or burned back, reproduces itself by sprouting from the stump.

The LEAVES are in clusters of two or three, from 3 to 5 inches long, slender, flexible, and dark blue-green. The CONES, or burrs, are the smallest of all our pines, 1½ to 2½ inches long, oblong, with small sharp prickles, generally clustered, and often holding to the twig for 3 or 4 years. The small seeds are mottled and have a wing, which is broadest near the center. The BARK is brownish red, broken into rectangular plates; it is thinner and lighter-colored than that of loblolly pine.

The WOOD of old trees is rather heavy and hard, of yellow-brown or orange color, fine-grained and less resinous than that of the other important southern pines. It is used largely for interior and exterior finishing, general construction, veneers, paper pulp, excelsior, cooperage, mine props, and other purposes.

7

LOBLOLLY PINE (*Pinus taeda* L.)

A fast-growing member of the yellow pine group, loblolly pine is found only in the southeastern part of the state and there only to a very limited extent. It is variously known locally as shortleaf pine, fox-tail pine and old-field pine. As the last name implies, it seeds

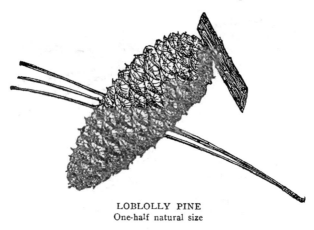

LOBLOLLY PINE
One-half natural size

up abandoned fields rapidly, particularly in sandy soils where the water is close to the surface. It is also frequent in clumps along the borders of swamps and as scattered specimens in the swamp hardwood forests.

The BARK is dark in color and deeply furrowed, and often attains a thickness of as much as 2 inches on large-sized trees. The LEAVES, or needles, 6 to 9 inches long, are borne three in a cluster, and, in the spring, bright green clumps of them at the ends of branches give a luxuriant appearance to the tree. The FRUIT is a cone, or burr, about 3 to 5 inches long, which ripens in the autumn of the second year, and during fall and early winter, sheds many seeds which, by their inch-long wings, are widely distributed by the wind.

The resinous WOOD is coarse-grained, with marked contrast, as in the other yellow pines, between the bands of early and late wood. The wood of second-growth trees has a wide range of uses where durability is not a requisite, such as for building material, box shooks, barrel staves, basket veneers, pulpwood, lath, mine props, piling and fuel.

8

PINON (Nut Pine)
(*Pinus edulis* Engelm.)

The nut pine, or pinon, is found in the western part of Cimarron county. The tree forms open forests over great areas from Colorado south and west into Mexico. It is a small tree found locally on warm slopes or in sheltered locations, and forms a bushy top with orange-colored branchlets.

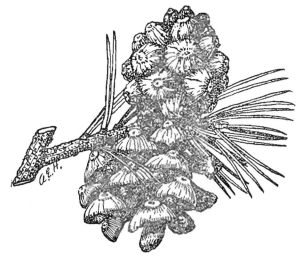

PINON (NUT PINE)
(*Pinus edulis* Engelm)

The LEAVES occur in clusters of 2 leaves each (rarely 3), and are stiff, stout, curved, dark green in color, and about an inch in length. Each year's crop remains on the tree from 5 to 8 years.

Like all the pines, it has male and female flowers separate on the same tree. The CONE, or burr, is rounded, about 1 to 2 inches across, and produces large seeds or "nuts," from ½ to ¾ inch long. The latter are rich in food values and form an important article of diet for the Indians. They are gathered and sold widely as a fancy "nut" in many larger towns and cities.

The WOOD is light, soft, close-grained, and pale brown, used for fuel and sometimes as fencing.

CYPRESS (Bald Cypress)
(*Taxodium distichum* Rich.)

The cypress, or bald cypress, is confined to the borders of streams tributary to the Red river in the southeastern part of the state. Its straight trunk with numerous ascending branches, and narrow conical outline makes the tree one of considerable beauty. In old age,

CYPRESS
One-half natural size

the tree generally has a broad fluted or buttressed base, a smooth, slowly tapering trunk and a broad, open, flat top of a few heavy branches and numerous small branchlets. The largest tree in the State is of this species. It is on Mountain Fork, nine miles east of Broken Bow, and measures about 9 feet in diameter and about 100 feet in height.

The BARK is silvery to cinnamon-red and finely divided by numerous longitudinal fissures. The LEAVES are about one-half to three-fourths of an inch in length, arranged in feather-like fashion along two sides of small branchlets, which fall in the autumn with the leaves still attached; or they are scale-like and much shorter, light green and sometimes silvery below.

The FRUIT is a rounded cone, or "ball," about one inch in diameter, consisting of thick, irregular scales.

The WOOD is light, soft, easily worked, varies in color from a light sapwood to dark-brown heartwood, and is particularly durable in contact with the soil. Hence it is in demand for exterior trim of buildings, greenhouse planking, boat and ship building, shingles, posts, poles and crossties.

For decorative planting, this species is a very desirable ornamental tree. It does not develop the "knees" when growing out of water, suggesting that these peculiar structures may serve as breathing organs for the roots.

RED CEDAR (*Juniperus virginiana* L.)

A very valuable tree found in all classes and conditions of soils---from swamp to dry rocky ridges---seeming to thrive on barren soils where few other trees are found. It is scattered throughout the State.

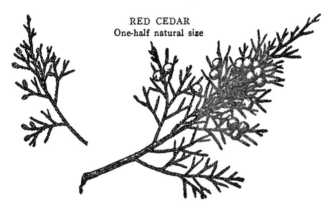

RED CEDAR
One-half natural size

There are two kinds of LEAVES, usually both kinds being found on the same tree. The commoner kind is dark green, minute and scale-like, clasping the stem in four ranks, so that the stems appear square. The other kind, usually appearing on young growth or various shoots, is awl-shaped, quite sharp-pointed, spreading and whitened.

The two kinds of FLOWERS are at the end of minute twigs on separate trees. Blooming in February or March, the male trees often assume a golden color from the small catkins, which, when shaken, shed clouds of yellow pollen. The FRUIT, which matures in one season, is pale blue, often with a white bloom, one-quarter of an inch in diameter, berry-like, enclosing one or two seeds in the sweet flesh. It is a favorite winter food for birds.

The BARK is very thin, reddish brown, peeling off in long, shred-like strips. The tree is extremely irregular in its growth, so that the trunk is usually more or less grooved.

The heart WOOD is distinctly red, and the sapwood white, this color combination making very striking effects when finished as cedar chests, closets and interior woodwork. The wood is aromatic, soft, strong and of even texture, and these qualities make it most desirable for lead pencils. It is very durable in contact with the soil, and on that account is in great demand for posts, poles and rustic work.

BLACK WALNUT (*Juglans nigra* L.)

This valuable forest tree occurs on rich bottom-lands and moist fertile hillsides in the eastern and southern parts of the State. In the forest, where it grows singly, it may attain a height of 100 feet with a

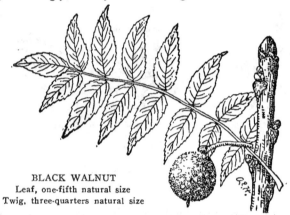

BLACK WALNUT
Leaf, one-fifth natural size
Twig, three-quarters natural size

straight stem, clear of branches for half its height. In open-grown trees the stem is short and the crown broad and spreading. Practically all of the large walnut has been cut in this State.

The LEAVES are alternate, compound, 1 to 2 feet long, consisting of from 15 to 23 leaflets of a yellowish green color. The leaflets are about 3 inches long, extremely tapering at the end, and toothed along the margin. The BARK is thick, dark brown in color, and divided by rather deep fissures into rounded ridges.

The FRUIT is a nut, borne singly or in pairs, and enclosed in a solid green husk which does not split open, even after the nut is ripe. The nut itself is black with a very hard, thick, finely ridged shell, enclosing a rich, oily kernel edible and highly nutritious.

The heart WOOD is of superior quality and value. It is heavy, hard and strong, and its rich chocolate brown color, freedom from warping and checking, susceptibility to a high polish, and durability make it highly prized for a great variety of uses, including furniture and cabinet work, gun-stocks, and airplane propellers. Small trees are mostly sapwood, which is light colored and not durable. Walnut is easily propagated from the nuts and grows rapidly on good soil, where it should be planted and grown for timber and nuts.

PECAN (*Hicoria pecan* (Marsh.) (Britton.) (*Carya pecan* Ashe and Gr.)

The pecan is found native for the most part south and east of a diagonal line drawn from the northeast to the southwest corner of the State, but extends north of this line east of Garfield and Grant counties. It makes an excellent shade tree, and has been planted considerably for this purpose and for its nuts. The

PECAN
One-quarter natural size

pecan is the largest of the hickories, attaining heights of over 100 feet and when grown in the open forming a large rounded top of symmetrical shape. The outer BARK is rough, hard, tight, but broken into scales; on the limbs, it is smooth at first but later tends to scale or divide as the bark grows old.

The LEAVES resemble those of the other hickories and the black walnut. They are made up of 9 to 17 leaflets, each oblong, toothed and long-pointed, and 4 to 8 inches long by about 2 inches wide.

The FLOWERS appear in early spring and hang in tassels from 2 to 3 inches long. The FRUIT is a nut, 4-winged or angled, pointed, from 1 to 2 inches long, and one-half to 1 inch in diameter, borne in a husk which divides along its grooved seams when the nut ripens in the fall. The nuts, which vary in size and in the thickness of the shell, have been greatly improved by selection and cultivation and are sold on the market in large quantities.

The WOOD is strong, tough, heavy and hard and is used occasionally in making handles and parts of vehicles, and for fuel.

13

BITTERNUT HICKORY
(*Hicoria minima* Britton)
(*Carya cordiformis* K. Koch)

The bitternut or pignut hickory is a tall slender tree with broadly pyramidal crown, attaining a height of 100 feet and a diameter of 2 to 3 feet. It is found in the eastrn part of the State on moist rich soils, but is nowhere very abundant.

Twig, one-half
natural size

BITTERNUT HICKORY
Leaf, one-third natural size

The BARK on the trunk is granite-gray, faintly tinged with yellow and less rough than in most of the hickories, yet broken into thin, plate-like scales. The winter buds are compressed, scurfy, bright yellow, quite different from those of its relatives.

The LEAVES are alternate, compound, from 6 to 10 inches long, and composed of from 7 to 11 leaflets. The individual leaflets are smaller and more slender than those of the other hickories.

The FLOWERS are of two kinds on the same tree. The FRUIT is about 1 inch long and thin-husked, while the nut is usually thin-shelled and brittle, and the kernel very bitter.

The WOOD is hard, strong and heavy, reddish brown in color. From this last fact it gets its local name of red hickory. It is said to be somewhat inferior to the other hickories, but is used for the same purposes.

14

NUTMEG HICKORY

(Hicoria myristicaeformis Michx.)
(Carya myristicaeformis Nuttall)

The nutmeg hickory is found only in rich soil on the borders of streams and swamps. It is restricted in its distribution, known in the State from the flood plains and swamp bottoms of the Red river, as far west as western Choctaw county, where it may attain a height of about 90 feet and a trunk diameter exceeding 2 feet. It is often known locally as the "blasted pecan."

The BARK is dark brown, tinged with red, one-half to three-quarters of an inch thick, with shallow fissures, the ridges separating into irregular, close, dark, reddish - brown scales.

The LEAVES are compound, 8 inches to over a foot in length, having 5 to 9 short stalked or nearly sessile leaflets. The leaflets are dark green above, more or less hairy and silvery white

NUTMEG HICKORY
Leaf, one-quarter natural size. Fruit, one-half natural size. Twig, two-thirds natural size

lustrous below, with a hairy midrib—a very striking feature, by which this species may be recognized.

The FRUIT, which is also distincive, is usually solitary 1½ inches long with four ridges to the base and covered with yellow-brown scurfy hairs. The husk is exceedingly thin, splitting nearly to the base. The NUT is ellipsoidal or sometimes slightly wider above the middle, pointed at the ends, and not flattened. The name applies to the nutmeg-like markings of gray streaks and spots on the surface of the reddish-brown nut, and to the thick and very hard bony shell. The seed is sweet.

The WOOD is hard, heavy, very strong, close grained and tough, of light brown color, with a thick layer of sapwood involving 80 to 90 annual-growth rings. It should be useful for manufactured parts where hickory is desirable.

This is a rare hickory of North America but rather frequent in the Red river bottoms.

15

SCALY-BARK OR SHELL-BARK HICKORY

(*Hicoria ovata* Britton)   (*Carya ovata* K. Koch)

The scaly-bark hickory is known by every child of the community because of its sweet and delicious nuts. It is a large commercial tree, averaging 60 to 100 feet high and 1 and 2 feet in diameter. It thrives best on rich, damp soil and is common along streams and on moist hillsides in the eastern part of the State.

Leaf, one-third
natural size

SCALY-BARK HICKORY
Twig, one-half natural size

The BARK of the trunk is rougher than on other hickories, light gray and separating into thick plates which are only slightly attached to the tree. The terminal winter buds are egg-shaped, the outer bud-scales having narrow tips.

The LEAVES are alternate, compound, from 8 to 15 inches long and composed of 5, rarely 7, obovate to ovate leaflets. The twigs are smooth or clothed with short hairs. The FRUIT is borne singly or in pairs, and is globular. The husk is thick and deeply grooved at the seams. The nut is much compressed and pale, the shell thin, and the kernel sweet. The FLOWERS are of two kinds, opening after the leaves have attained nearly their full size.

The WOOD is heavy, hard, tough and very strong. It is used largely in the manufacture of agricultural implements and tool handles, and in the building of carriages and wagons. For fuel the hickories are the most satisfactory of our native trees.

KING NUT HICKORY (Big Shell-Bark)
(*Hicoria laciniosa* Michx.   *Carya laciniosa* Schn.)

The king nut hickory becomes a very large tree and is found in the rich bottom land forests of the northeastern part of the State, usually in soil inundated during a part of the year. This tree may attain a height well over 100 feet in a straight slender trunk,

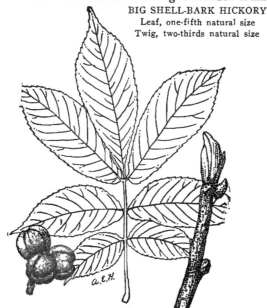

BIG SHELL-BARK HICKORY
Leaf, one-fifth natural size
Twig, two-thirds natural size

not generally exceeding 3 feet in diameter, free from branches for a height of 60 feet. This species is often confused with the scaly-bark hickory, which it resembles, except for its larger size. King nut is distinguished also by its somewhat hairy orange-colored branchlets, the thick bony shell of its nut, and the larger number of leaflets.

The BARK is light gray, 1 to 2 inches thick, separating into plates as much as 4 feet long and clinging to the trunk for many years. The winter buds are large, sometimes an inch long and two-thirds of an inch wide.

The LEAVES are 15 to 22 inches long, compound, with 5 to 9 leaflets, the petioles often remaining attached to the branches through the winter.

The FRUIT is borne solitary or in pairs, is very large, nearly globular, slightly depressed at the apex, with a woody husk a fourth inch or more in thickness, brown at maturity, containing one or occasionally two nuts, 2 to 2½ inches long, about 1¾ inches wide and flattened, with a bony shell about one-fourth inch thick.

The WOOD is dark brown, very hard and tough, close grained and very flexible, with a fairly narrow zone of white sapwood.

17

WHITEHEART OR WHITE HICKORY
(MOCKERNUT HICKORY)
(*Hicoria alba* Britton)   (*Carya alba* K. Koch)

The white hickory, whiteheart, mockernut, or big-bud hickory is common on well-drained soils in the eastern part of the State. It is a tall, short-limbed tree averaging 60 feet high and 1 to 2 feet in diameter.

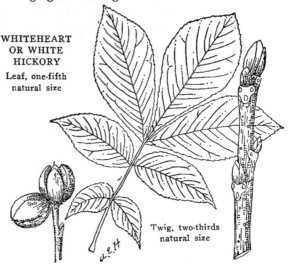

WHITEHEART
OR WHITE
HICKORY
Leaf, one-fifth
natural size

Twig, two-thirds
natural size

The BARK is dark gray, hard, closely and deeply furrowed, often apparently cross-furrowed or netted. The winter buds are large, round or broadly egg-shaped, and covered with downy, hard scales. The recent shoots are short, stout and more or less covered with a downy growth.

The LEAVES are large, strong-scented and hairy, composed of 7 to 9 obovate to oblong, pointed leaflets which turn a beautiful yellow in the fall.

The FLOWERS, like those of all other hickories, are of two kinds on the same tree; the male in three-branched catkins, the female in clusters of 2 to 5. The FRUIT is oval, nearly round or slightly pear-shaped with a very thick, strong-scented husk which splits nearly to the base when ripe. The nut is of various forms, but is sometimes 4 to 6 ridged, light brown, and has a very thick shell and small, sweet kernel.

The WOOD is heavy, hard, tough and strong; it is white excepting the comparatively small, dark-brown heart, hence the name white hickory. It is used for vehicle parts, handles and picker-sticks. It furnishes the best of fuel. This and the other hickories are very desirable both for forest and shade trees.

BLACK HICKORY

(*Hicoria Buckleyi* Dur. varieties)
(*Carya Buckleyi* Dur. varieties)

This is the most common hickory of the Ozark region. It is found on rocky hillsides or on sandy upland, and is distinguished by its obovoid fruit, and by its rusty brown hairs found on the young leaves and branches. It forms a tree 60 to 75 feet high, with a trunk 2 feet in diameter.

BLACK HICKORY
Leaf, one-quarter natural size.
Fruit, one-third and Twig,
three-quarters natural size.

The BARK is dark gray or nearly black, deeply divided into rough ridges, or it may be irregularly fissured and separating into thin scales. The winter buds are ovoid and covered with rusty hairs mixed with silvery scales.

The LEAVES are 8 to 12 inches long with 5 to 7, usually 7, leaflets and with rusty-hairy slender leafstalks. The leaves are dark green, lustrous above, and much paler beneath. The FLOWERS are similar to other hickories.

The FRUIT is obovoid, narrowed or abruptly contracted into a short stalk at the base with a husk one-twelfth to one-sixth inch thick, splitting to the middle or nearly to the base. The NUT is nearly obovoid to oblong rounded at the ends, compressed and slightly four-angled with a shell one-sixth to one-fifth inch thick. The seed is sweet.

The WOOD is hard and brittle, used chiefly for fuel.

19

BLACK WILLOW
(*Salix nigra* Marsh.)

The black willow is found along streams throughout the State. It rarely grows to be over 50 feet in height and is frequently found growing singly or in clumps along the water courses. In winter the easily separable, bright reddish-brown or golden, naked twigs are quite conspicuous.

The LEAVES are from 3 to 6 inches long and less than one-half a n i n c h wide; the tips are very much tapered and the entire margins finely toothed. The leaves are bright green on both sides, turning pale yellow in the early autumn.

The FLOWERS are in catkins, the male and female on separate trees. The FRUIT is a pod bearing numerous minute seeds which are furnished with long silky down, enabling them to be blown long distances.

The BARK is deeply divided into broad, flat ridges which separate into t h i c k plate-like s c a l e s. On old trees it becomes very shaggy. In color it varies from light brown tinged with orange to dark brown or nearly black.

The WOOD is soft, light and not strong. A high grade of charcoal, used in the manufacture of gunpowder, is obtained from willow wood, and it is the chief wood used in the manufacture of artificial limbs.

BLACK WILLOW
Two-thirds natural size

There are many species, or kinds, of willows not easily distinguished. They are of high value in checking soil erosion and waste along stream banks, for which purpose they should be more extensively grown.

In eastern Oklahoma Ward's Willow (**Salix longipes** var. **wardi** Schn.), a variety with leaves pale on the lower surface, sometimes becomes a tree but more commonly it is only a shrub.

CAROLINA POPLAR (COTTONWOOD)
(*Populus deltoides* Marsh.)

The cottonwood, or Carolina poplar, is found along streams throughout the State. The tree is easily propagated by cuttings and grows rapidly, hence it has been widely planted to get shade quickly. For this purpose, however, the tree is unsatisfactory, because it begins to shed the leaves by midsummer, the "cotton" from

CAROLINA POPLAR
Leaf, one-half natural size.   Twig, one-third natural size.

the female, or seed-bearing tree is often a nuisance, the soft wood is easily broken by winds, and the rank growth of the roots often results in stopping drain pipes and cracking and lifting sidewalks.

The LEAVES are simple, alternate, broadly ovate or triangular, pointed, square at the base, and coarsely toothed on the edges, 3 to 5 inches across each way, covered with soft white hairs on the under side, supported by flattened slender stems, 2 to 3 inches long, The winter buds are covered with chestnut-brown, resinous scales. The FLOWERS are in catkins of two kinds, male and female, and appear before the leaves. The FRUIT containing the seed has a cluster of white silky hairs, which carries it for long distances.

The WOOD is soft, light-weight, warps easily upon drying, but is used for many purposes, sometimes as a substitute for yellow poplar and linden. It makes the highest grade of gloss magazine paper for the printing of half-tone illustrations.

21

RIVER BIRCH (Red Birch) (*Betula nigra* L.)

This is the only native birch found at low elevations in the South. It is at home, as the name implies, along water courses, and inhabits the deep, rich soils along the borders of streams, ponds, lakes, and swamps which are sometimes inundated for weeks at a time. It is found in the eastern part of the State.

RIVER BIRCH
One-third natural size

The BARK provides a ready means of distinguishing this tree. It varies from reddish brown to cinnamon-red in color, and peels back in tough papery layers. These layers persist on the trunk, representing a very ragged and quite distinctive appearance. Unlike the bark of our other birches, the thin papery layers are usually covered with a gray powder. On older trunks, deeply furrowed, and of a reddish-brown color.

The LEAVES are simple, alternate, 2 to 3 inches long, more or less oval in shape, with double-toothed edges. The upper surface is dark green and the lower a pale yellowish green.

The FLOWERS are in catkins, the two kinds growing on the same tree. The FRUIT is cone-shaped about 1 inch long, and densely crowded with little winged nutlets that ripen from May to June.

The WOOD is strong and fairly close-grained. It has been to some extent used in the manufacture of woodenware, in turnery and for wagon hubs. Since, however, this tree is scattered in its distribution and mostly confined to the banks of streams, it does not figure largely in commercial lumbering, but is cut chiefly for firewood.

BEECH (*Fagus grandifolia* Ehrh.)

The beech occurs only in the eastern part of the State where it is infrequently found scattered with oaks and hickories on rich, well-drained bottoms. It is one of the most beautiful of all trees, either in summer or winter.

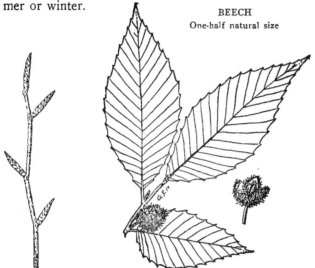

BEECH
One-half natural size

The simple, oval LEAVES are 3 to 4 inches long, pointed at the tip, and coarsely toothed along the margin. When mature, they are almost leathery in texture. The beech produces a dense shade. The winter buds are long, slender and pointed.

The BARK is, perhaps, the most distinctive characteristic, as it maintains an unbroken, light gray surface throughout its life. So tempting is this smooth expanse to the owner of a jackknife that the beech has been well designated the "initial tree."

The little, brown, three-sided beech NUTS are almost as well known as chestnuts. They form usually in pairs in a prickly burr. The kernel is sweet and edible, but so small as to offer insufficient reward for the pains of biting open the thin-shelled husk.

The WOOD of the beech is very hard, strong, and tough, though it will not last long on exposure to weather or in the soil. The tree is of no great economic importance as a lumber tree, though the wood is used to some extent for furniture, flooring, carpenters' tools, and novelty wares.

23

CHINQUAPIN (*Castanea ozarkensis Ashe*)

This small tree occurs at rare intervals in the eastern part of the State on both lowlands and dry uplands, but is most frequently found in the higher mountains. It is usually under 10 inches in diameter and less than 30 feet high. The trunk is short and straight and bears a rounded head made up of slender, spreading branches. Sometimes the small trees, less than 10 feet in height, form dense thickets.

CHINQUAPIN

Twig, one-third natural size.   Leaf, one-half natural size.

The LEAVES, BARK and FRUIT resemble those of the common chestnut, and the fruit ripens in the late summer or fall. The nut, however, is borne singly in a burr that measures commonly only a little more than an inch in diameter. The nut is rounded, dark chestnut-brown, shiny, and the thin coat, lined inside with fine whitish hairs, contains a sweet kernel, which is prized for food.

The WOOD is light, hard, strong, coarse-grained; it is suitable for fence posts, crossties, and fuel; but, because of its small size and comparative scarcity, it is of little economic importance.

IRONWOOD (Hop Hornbeam)
(*Ostrya virginiana* K. Koch)

The tree gets its common names from the qualities of its wood and the hop-like fruit. It is a small, slender, generally round-topped tree, from 20 to 30 feet high and 7 to 10 inches in diameter. The top consists of long slender branches, commonly drooping toward the ends. It is found mostly on rather dry soils throughout the upland and mountain region of the eastern part of the State.

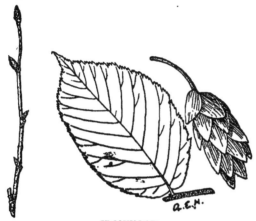

IRONWOOD

Twig, one-half natural size.   Leaf, one-third natural size.

The BARK is mostly light brown or reddish brown, and finely divided into thin scales by which the tree, after a little acquaintance, can be easily recognized.

The LEAVES are simple, alternate, generally oblong with narrowed tips, sharply toothed along the margin, sometimes doubly toothed, from 2 to 3 inches long.

The FLOWERS are of two kinds on the same tree; the male, in drooping catkins which form the previous summer, the female, in erect catkins on the newly formed twigs. The FRUIT, which resembles that of the common hop vine, consists of a branch of leafy bracts 1 to 2 inches long containing a number of flattened ribbed nutlets.

The WOOD is strong, hard, durable, light brown to white, with thick pale sapwood. Often used for handles of tools, mallets and other small articles.

25

HORNBEAM
(*Carpinus caroliniana* Walt.)

The hornbeam, often known as ironwood and occasionally as blue or water beech, is a small, slow-growing, bushy tree with a spreading top of slender, crooked, or drooping branches. It is found along streams and in low ground in the eastern part of the State. Its height is usually from 20 to 30 feet and its diameter 4 to 8 inches, although it sometimes grows larger.

The trunk is fluted with irregular ridges extending up and down the tree. The BARK is light brownish gray to dark bluish gray in color, sometimes marked with dark bands, extending horizontally on the trunk.

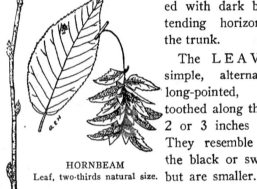

HORNBEAM

Leaf, two-thirds natural size.

Twig, one-half natural size.

The LEAVES are simple, alternate, oval, long-pointed, doubly toothed along the margin, 2 or 3 inches in length. They resemble those of the black or sweet birch, but are smaller.

The FLOWERS are borne in catkins separately on the same tree; the male catkin about 1½ inches long, the female about three-fourths of an inch, with small, leaf-like, 3-lobed green scales. The FRUIT is a nut about one-third of an inch long. It falls, attached to the leaf-like scale which acts as a wing in aiding its distribution by the wind.

The WOOD is tough, close-grained, heavy and strong. It is sometimes selected for use for levers, tool handles, wooden cogs, mallets, wedges, etc. The tree is of little commercial importance and often occupies space in the woods that should be utilized by more valuable kinds.

WHITE OAK (*Quercus alba* L.)

Within its natural range, which includes practically the entire eastern half of the United States, the white oak is one of the most important timber trees. It commonly reaches a height of 60 to 100 feet and a diameter of 2 to 3 feet; sometimes it becomes much larger. It is found in a wide variety of soils. When grown in a dense stand it has a straight continuous trunk, free of side branches for over half its height. In the open, however, the tree develops a broad crown with far-reaching limbs. Well-grown specimens are strikingly beautiful.

WHITE OAK
Leaf, one-quarter natural size.
Twig, one-half natural size.

The LEAVES are alternate, simple, 5 to 9 inches long and about half as broad. They are deeply divided into 5 to 9 rounded, finger-like lobes. The young leaves are a soft silvery gray or yellow or red while unfolding, becoming later bright green above and much paler below. The nut is three-quarters to one inch long, light brown, about one-quarter enclosed in the warty cup. It is relished by hogs and other livestock. The BARK is thin, light ashy gray and covered with loose scales or broad plates.

The WOOD is useful and valuable. It is heavy, strong, hard, tough, close-grained, durable, and light brown in color. The uses are many, including construction, shipbuilding, tight cooperage, furniture, wagons, implements, interior finish, flooring, and fuel. Notwithstanding its rather slow growth, white oak is valuable for forest, highway and ornamental planting.

SWAMP WHITE OAK

(*Quercus bicolor* Wild., formerly *Q. platanoides* Sudw.)

The swamp white oak, as the name implies, inhabits the low grounds and bottom lands, and in general appearance is much like that of the true white oak. It is found chiefly in the northeastern part of the State, in association with several other oaks, maples, ash and hickories.

The BARK is deeply and irregularly divided by fissures into broad ridges of a grayish-brown color.

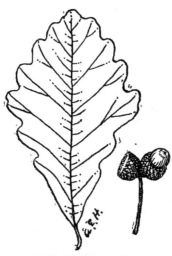

SWAMP WHITE OAK
One-half natural size

The LEAVES are generally broader at or beyond the middle length (pear-shaped) and wedge-shaped toward the base, wavy and indented along the margin, dark green and shiny above and grayish and fuzzy beneath, and 5 to 6 inches in length by 2 to 4 inches in width. The chestnut oak and swamp chestnut oak have leaves somewhat similar, but acorns of different shape and larger.

The acorn, or FRUIT, occurs commonly in pairs and requires only one season to mature. It is borne on slender stalks from 2 to 4 inches in length. The nut, or acorn proper is about 1 inch long by two-thirds of an inch thick and enclosed for about one-third its length in a thick narrow-shaped cup.

The WOOD is heavy, hard, strong and tough, and used for similar purposes as the true white oak, such as furniture, cabinet work, flooring, cooperage, ties, fence posts and fuel.

28

POST OAK
(*Quercus stellata* Wang., formerly *Q. minor* Sarg.)

The post oak is usually a medium-sized tree, with a rounded crown, commonly reaching a height of 50 to 60 feet and a diameter of 1 to 2 feet, but sometimes considerably larger. It occurs throughout the eastern

POST OAK
One-third natural size.

half of the State and is scattered over parts of the western half. It is most abundant on the poorer soils.

The BARK is rougher and darker than the white oak and broken into smaller scales. The stout young twigs and the leaves are coated at first with a thick light-colored fuzz which soon becomes darker and later drops away entirely.

The LEAVES are usually 4 to 5 inches long and nearly as broad, deeply 5-lobed with broad rounded divisions, the lobes broadest at the ends. They are thick and somewhat leathery, dark green and shiny on the upper surface, lighter green and rough hairy beneath.

The FLOWERS, like those of the other oaks, are of two kinds on the same tree, the male in drooping, clustered catkins, the female inconspicuous. The FRUIT is an oval acorn, one-half to 1 inch long, set in a rather small cup which may or may not be stalked.

The WOOD is very heavy, hard, close-grained, light to dark brown, durable in contact with the soil. It is used for crossties and fence posts, and along with other oaks of the white oak class for furniture and other purposes.

29

BURR OAK (Mossy Cup Oak)
(*Quercus macrocarpa* Michx.)

The burr oak occurs throughout the State except in the Panhandle, in rich bottom lands along streams, or even on rich hillsides along spring-fed ravines. The name alludes to the fringe around the cup of the acorn, which is sometimes very large. The tree usually has a broad top of heavy spreading branches and a relatively

BURR OAK
One-third natural size.

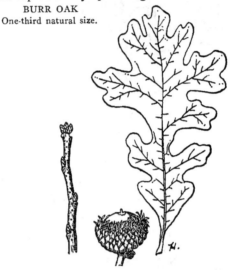

short body. In maturity, it attains a diameter of 5 feet or more and a height of over 80 feet.

The BARK is light-gray and is usually broken up into small narrow flakes. The burr oak does not often form a part of the forest stand, as do some other oaks, but occurs generally singly in open stands in fields. It requires a moist but well-drained soil.

The LEAVES resemble somewhat those of the common white oak, but are much larger and have a pair of deep indentations on their border near the base, and wavy notches on the broad middle and upper portions of the leaf. They range from 6 to 12 inches long and 3 to 6 inches wide. The FRUIT, or acorn, is a nut set deeply in the fringed cup. It is usually 1 inch or much more in diameter but varies widely in respect to size and the degree to which the nut is inclosed in the mossy fringed cup.

The WOOD is heavy, hard, strong, tough and durable. It is used for much the same purposes as the other white oaks—for lumber, crossties, and fuel.

CHINQUAPIN OAK (CHINQUAPIN, PIN OAK)
(*Quercus muhlenbergii* Engelm., formerly
Q. acuminata Sarg.)

This oak, which is an excellent timber tree, occurs throughout the eastern part of the State and as far west as Caddo county. It grows on practically all classes of soil and in all moisture conditions except in swamps, and is a very tenacious tree on shallow, dry soil. The BARK is light gray, and breaks up into short narrow flakes on the main trunk and old limbs.

CHINQUAPIN OAK
One-third natural size.

It reaches a height of 20 to 50 feet. The straight shapely trunk bears a round-topped head composed of small branches, which makes it an attractive shade tree.

The LEAVES are oblong, 3 to 6 inches in length, 1½ to 3 inches wide, and equally toothed or notched on the edges, resembling the leaves of the chestnut oak. The FRUIT, which ripens in the fall of the first season, is light to dark brown when ripe, and edible if roasted. This acorn is from one-half to nearly an inch long, usually less than one inch in diameter, and is set in a shallow cup.

The WOOD is heavy, very hard, tough, strong, durable, and takes an excellent polish. It is used in manufacturing lumber and timbers, crossties, fence posts and fuel. A portion of the lumber no doubt goes into furniture.

SWAMP CHESTNUT OAK
(Basket Oak, or Cow Oak)
(*Quercus prinus* L., formerly *Q. michauxii Nutt.*)

This tree is distinguished from the preceding by having a broader leaf, by its larger fruit, by the short stalk bearing the acorns which is sometimes one-half inch long or as long as the leaf stalk and by the fact that it occurs in its greatest abundance in bottom lands.

In the appearance of its bark and branches it closely resembles the ordinary white oak, but may be distinguished by means of the leaf and large acorn. The tree attains heights of about 100 feet and diameters of about 4 feet.

SWAMP CHESTUNT OAK
Leaf, One-third Natural Size.
Twig, One-half natural size.

The L E A V E S are oval, broader towards the point and notched on the edge somewhat like the chinquapin oak, but r o u n d e d instead of pointed. They v a r y from 4 to 8 inches in length, are downy beneath and turn a rich crimson in the fall. The BARK is a very light gray, and on old trees is broken into broad flakes or divided into strips.

The acorn, or FRUIT, attains a diameter of more than an inch and a length of 1½ inches. The acorn, which is a bright shiny brown and set in a rather shallow cup, is considerably larger than that of the white oak. It is frequently eaten by cows and this fact gives the tree one of its common names.

The WOOD is heavy, hard, tough, strong, and takes an excellent polish. It is used in manufacturing lumber, veneer, boards (shakes), tight cooperage; for fuel and fence posts; and extensively for making baskets.

NORTHERN RED OAK
(Quercus borealis maxima Ashe.,
formerly *Q. rubra* L.)

The northern red oak occurs in the eastern part of the State, but is most common and of best quality in the mountains. It is sometimes called "mountain water oak" and is not found in swamps. It usually attains a height of about 70 feet and a diameter ranging from 2 to 3 feet, but is sometimes much larger. The forest-grown tree is tall and straight with a clear trunk and narrow crown.

The BARK on young stems is smooth, gray to brown, on older trees thick and broken by shallow fissures into regular, flat, smooth-surfaced plates.

LEAVES are simple, alternate 5 to 9 inches long and 4 to 6 inches wide, broader toward the tip, divided into 7 to 9 lobes, each lobe being somewhat coarsely toothed and firm, bristle-tipped, dull green above, paler below, often turning a brilliant red after frost.

NORTHERN RED OAK
Leaf, one-third natural size.
Twig, one-half natural size.

The FLOWERS, as in all the oaks, are of two kinds on the same tree, the male in long, drooping, clustered catkins, opening with the leaves, the female solitary or slightly clustered. The FRUIT is a large acorn maturing the second year. The nut is from three-fourths to 1¾ inches long, blunt-topped, flat at base, with only its base inclosed in the very shallow dark-brown cup.

The WOOD is hard, strong, coarse-grained, with light reddish-brown heartwood and thin lighter-colored sapwood. It is used for cooperage, interior finish, construction, furniture, and crossties. Because of its average rapid growth, high-grade wood, and general freedom from insect and fungus attack, it should be widely planted in the higher portions of the State for timber production and as a shade tree.

SOUTHERN RED OAK

(Quercus rubra Linn., formerly *Q. digitata* Sudw.)

The southern red oak, commonly known as red oak and referred to in books as Spanish oak, usually grows to a height of 70 to 80 feet and a diameter of 2 to 3 feet, though larger trees are not infrequently found. It is found in the eastern part of the State. Its large spreading branches form a broad, round, open top. The BARK is rough, though not deeply furrowed, and varies from light gray on younger trees to dark gray or almost black on older ones.

SOUTHERN RED OAK
Leaf, one-third natural size.
Twig, one-half natural size.

The LEAVES are of two different types: (1) irregular-shaped lobes, mostly narrow, bristle-tipped, the central lobe often the longest; or (2) pear-shaped with 3 rounded lobes at the outer end. They are dark lustrous green above and gray down beneath, the contrast being strikingly seen in a wind or rain storm.

The FLOWERS appear in April while the leaves are unfolding. The FRUIT ripens the second year. The small rounded acorn, about half an inch long, is set in a thin saucer-shaped cup which tapers to a short stem.

The WOOD is heavy, hard, strong, coarse-grained, and is less subject to defects than most other red oaks. It is used for rough lumber and for furniture, chairs, tables, etc. It is a desirable timber tree, especially on the poorer, drier soils. The bark is rich in tannin.

The freedom of this tree from disease, its thrifty growth, large handsome form and long life make it very desirable for shade or ornamental use.

BLACK OAK

(Quercus velutina Lam.)

The black oak usually grows to be about 60 feet in height and 1 to 3 feet in diameter. It is found in the eastern part of the State on dry plains and ridges but seldom on rich ground. The crown is irregularly shaped and wide, with a clear trunk for 20 feet or more on large trees.

The BARK on the very young trunks is smooth and dark brown but soon becomes thick and black, with deep furrows and rough broken ridges. The bright-yellow color and bitter taste of the inner bark, due to tannic acid, are distinguishing characteristics.

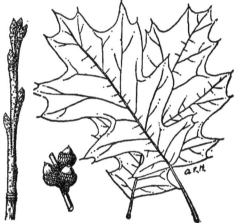

BLACK OAK
Twig, one-half natural size.   Leaf, one-third natural size.

The LEAVES are alternate, simple, 5 to 10 inches long, and 3 to 8 inches wide, shallow or deeply lobed, the shape varying greatly. When mature, the leaves are dark green and shiny on the upper surface, pale on the lower, more or less covered with down, and with conspicuous rusty brown hairs in the forks of the veins.

The FRUIT matures the second season. The light-brown nut is from one-half to 1 inch long, more or less hemispherical in shape, and from one-half to three-quarters inclosed in the thin, dark-brown, scaly cup. The kernel is yellow and extremely bitter.

The WOOD is hard, heavy, strong, coarse-grained and checks easily. It is a bright red-brown with a thin outer edge of paler sapwood. It is used for the same purposes as red oak, under which name it is put on the market. Its growth is rather slow.

SPOTTED OAK (TEXAS OAK)
(*Quercus shumardii* Buckl., formerly *Q. texana* Sarg.)

This tree, sometimes confused with northern red oak, Spanish oak and black oak, is found in the eastern part of the State on well-drained alluvial soils, and on mountain slopes, especially on limestone soils. It forms a tall, wide-spreading, rather open head. The

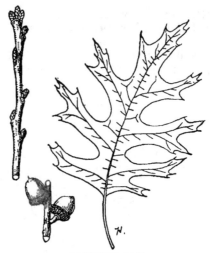

SPOTTED OAK
Twig, one-half natural size.   Leaf, one-third natural size.

BARK is dark, rough, divided into ridges, and usually from 1 to 1½ inches thick. It does not usually compose the principal part of any forest stand, but it more often occurs as individuals. It attains a diameter of over 3 feet and a height of more than 100 feet but is usually much smaller.

The LEAVES are simple, alternate, 6 to 8 inches long by 4 to 5 inches wide, mostly seven-lobed, and each one slightly lobed or deep-toothed. They resemble those of the scarlet oak and are smaller and more deeply lobed than those of the black oak.

The FRUIT is a small acorn, about two-thirds of an inch in diameter and three-quarters of an inch long, set in a shallow cup.

The WOOD is heavy, hard, strong, close-grained, and light reddish brown in color. It is used much as other red oak.

In the upland portions of the State the variety schneckii Sarg. is the common form which has a rougher, dark-grayish bark and deeper cups to the acorns.

BLACK JACK OAK
(Quercus marilandica Muench.)

The occurrence of blackjack oak is said to indicate poor soil. It is certain that it often occurs on dry or poorly drained gravely, clay, or sandy upland soils where few other forest trees thrive. This perhaps accounts chiefly for its slow rate of growth. It is found in most parts of the State that support a natural tree

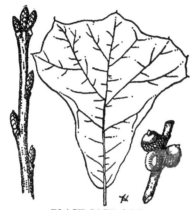

BLACK JACK OAK
Twig, two-thirds natural size.   Leaf, one-third natural size.

growth. The tree sometimes reaches a height of 50 or 60 feet and a diameter of 16 inches, but it is usually much smaller. Its hard, stiff, drooping branches form a dense crown which usually contains many persistent dead twigs. The BARK is rough, very dark, often nearly black, and broken into small, hard scales or flakes.

The LEAVES are of leathery texture, dark green on the upper surface, lighter underneath, broadly wedge-shaped, 4 to 10 inches long and about the same in width. The FRUIT is an acorn about three-quarters of an inch long, yellow-brown and often striped, inclosed for half its length or more in a thick light-brown cup.

The WOOD is heavy, hard and strong; when used at all, it is used mostly as firewood.

WATER OAK
(*Quercus nigra* L.)

The water oak is found native along the borders of swamps and streams and on rich bottom lands in the eastern part of the State. It has been widely planted in the Southern States along streets and in parks as a shade tree. When fully grown this tree reaches a height of about 80 feet and a diameter of from 1 to over 3 feet. The trunk is shapely. The BARK is s m o o t h, light brown tinged with red, and has many smooth t h i n scales over the surface. The water oak çan be most readily distinguished f r o m the willow oak---a close associate, but longer lived---by the differences i n t h e general s h a p e and size of the leaves.

WATER OAK

Leaf, one-third natural size.
Twig, one-half natural size.

The LEAVES are simple, quite variable in shape, mostly oblong, broader near the point, and narrower at the base, giving a wedge-shaped effect. They are usually slightly three-lobed, at the outer end, thin, and of a dull bluish-green color, paler below than above; mostly smooth, and usually 2 to 3 inches long and 1 to 1½ inches wide; they remain green for some time and gradually fall from the tree during the winter.

The FLOWERS appear in April when the leaves are beginning to unfold. The FRUIT, or acorn, matures at the end of the second season. The acorn is from one-half to two-thirds of an inch in length and nearly as broad, light brown or yellowish brown and often striped, inclosed at the base only in a thin saucer-shaped cup.

The WOOD is heavy, hard, and strong, light brown in color, with lighter-colored sapwood. It is not used to a great extent as lumber, but the trees are cut and utilized for piling, crossties, and fuel.

WILLOW OAK (*Quercus phellos* L.)

The willow oak, often called water oak, occurs in the eastern part of the State, except on the higher slopes and mountains. It is most often found in lowlands and along the borders of rivers and swamps, but often also on rich sandy uplands. It is a beautiful and long-lived tree, and desirable for roadsides, lawns and parks, for which it has been widely planted.

The slender willow-like LEAVES, on a tree whose habit of growth is manifestly that of an oak, make the tree easy to identify in the forest. The leaves are 2 to 4 inches long and one-half to 1 inch wide, with smooth or slightly wavy margin, b r i s t l e-pointed, smooth, light green and shiny above, but dull and usually smooth below; alternate in arrangement on the twig and borne on a short stout stem. The BARK is generally smooth and of a reddish brown color; with age, the bark becomes slightly roughened and divided by narrow ridges.

WILLOW OAK
Twig, one-half natural size.
Leaf, one-third natural size.

The small ACORNS, closely set along the stem, mature at the end of the second year. The nut is a light-brown hemisphere, about one-half an inch in diameter, its base scarcely enclosed in the shallow, reddish-brown cup. The nuts are eaten as food by bluejays, grackles ("black birds"), and several other species of birds, as well as by rodents.

The WOOD is not separated commercially from other species in the red oak group. It is heavy, strong, rather coarse-grained, light brown tinged with red, and not durable when exposed to the weather. It is used locally for crossties, bridge planks, barn sills, and general construction.

SHIN OAK
(*Quercus mohriana* Rydb.)

A small tree with spreading or bushy top, the shin oak is one representative of a group of oaks characteristic of the semi-arid Southwest. It is found in the western part of the main body of Oklahoma, and in the extreme western end of the Panhandle.

The BARK is thin, and deeply furrowed and rough. The LEAVES are 2 to 4 inches long by about an

SHIN OAK
(*Ouercus mohrinana* Rydb)

inch wide, oblong, with wavy or toothed edges, thick, and gray green in color.

The male flowers, or aments, are in short pendant clusters, and the female very small. Like all of the white oak group, the FRUIT, or acorn, ripens in one season. Its cup encloses the small rounded nut for about one-half of its length, and is much thicker and rougher at the base than at the top or outer edge. The acorns form in pairs or singly and are attached closely to the branchlets.

The WOOD is of little commercial importance, used mostly for firewood. It has not been studied to any great degree, chiefly because of the small size of the tree and its general inferiority to that of some of the other oaks.

WHITE ELM (American Elm)
(*Ulmus americana* L.)

The famous shade tree of New England, whose range, however, extends to the Rocky Mountains and southward to Texas. Within this vast area, it is generally common except in the high mountains and wet bottom lands. It reaches an average height of 60 to 70 feet and a diameter of 2 to 3 feet. The BARK is dark gray, divided into irregular, flat-topped, thick ridges, and is generally firm, though on old trees it tends to come off in flakes. An incision into the inner bark will show alternate layers of brown and white.

The LEAVES are alternate, simple, 4 to

Twig, one-half natural size.

WHITE ELM
Leaf, one-third natural size.

6 inches long, rather thick, somewhat one-sided, doubly toothed on the margin, and generally smooth above and downy below. The leaf veins are very pronounced and run in parallel lines from the midrib to leaf-edge.

The FLOWERS are small, perfect, greenish, on slender stalks sometimes an inch long, appearing before the leaves in very early spring. The FRUIT is a light green, oval shaped samara (winged fruit) with the seed portion in the center and surrounded entirely by a wing. A deep notch in the end of the wing is distinctive of the species. The seed ripens in the spring and by its wing is widely disseminated by the wind.

The WOOD is heavy, hard, strong, tough, and difficult to split. It is used for hubs of wheels, saddle trees, boats and ships, barrel hoops, and veneer for baskets and crates.

Because of its spreading fan-shaped form, graceful pendulous branches, and long life, the white elm justly holds its place as one of the most desirable shade trees.

WINGED ELM
(*Ulmus alata* Michx.)

The winged elm gets its common name from the thin corky growth or "wings," usually found on the smaller branches. On large rapidly-growing trees the wings are often absent. It is found in the eastern part of the State, extending west to Garfield county, usually on dry uplands, but often in moist soils along streams and in waste places. It grows rapidly in moist situations, and at the same time is one of the best trees

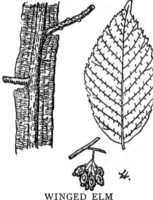

WINGED ELM
Two-thirds natural size.

for planting along roadsides in dry poor locations. It is comparatively free from disease, though not notably long-lived. This elm is a medium-sized tree of 40 to 50 feet in height and rarely as large as 2 feet in diameter. It forms a rather open, round-topped head.

The BARK is light brown, tinged with red, and divided into irregular flat ridges and fissures.

The LEAVES are simple, alternate, 2 to 4 inches long and 1 to 2 inches broad, coarsely double-toothed, thick, dark green and smooth above, and pale and softly downy below. They are small and pointed at the tip, which distinguishes them from the small blunt leaves of the cedar elm.

The FLOWERS appear in early spring, long before the leaves unfold. The FRUIT ripens in the spring about the time the leaves appear; it is winged, tipped with two small incurved awns or beaks, oblong, reddish brown, about one-third of an inch long, with a long slender stalk at the base, and covered with white hairs.

The WOOD is very similar to that of the other elms ---heavy, hard, strong and difficult to split. It is occasionally used for hubs and mauls. Formerly, rope made of the inner bark was used for binding the covers to cotton bales.

The red elm, **Ulmus serotina** Sarg., becomes a large tree usually growing on river banks or on protected north slopes along high limestone cliffs in the mountains. It has leaves intermediate in size between the winged elm and the white elm, corky ridges on some of the twigs, and flowers in the autumn

SLIPPERY ELM (Red Elm) (*Ulmus fulva* Michx.)

The slippery elm, or red elm, is found in the eastern and southern parts of the State. It is found principally on the banks of streams and on low hillsides in rich soil. It is a tree of small to moderate size, but noticeably wide-spreading. It is usually less than 40 feet in height and 6 inches in diameter, although trees of larger dimensions are occasionally found.

The BARK on the trunk is frequently 1 inch thick, dark grayish brown, and broken by shallow fissures into flat ridges. The inner bark is used to some extent for medicinal purposes, as it is fragrant, and, when chewed, affords a slippery, mucilaginous s u b s t a n ce, whence the tree gets its name.

SLIPPERY ELM
Leaf, one-third natural size.

Twig, one-half natural size

The LEAVES are simple, alternate on the stem, 4 to 6 inches in l e n g t h, sharp-pointed, their bases unsymmetrical, doubly-toothed on the edges, thick, dark green, and rough on both sides.

The FRUIT consists of a seed surrounded by a thin, broad, greenish wing, about one-half an inch in diameter; the FLOWERS appear in early spring and the fruit ripens when the leaves are about half-grown.

The WOOD is close-grained, tough, strong, heavy, hard, moderately durable in contact with the soil. It is used for fence-posts, crossties, agricultural implements, ribs for small boats and for some other purposes.

WATER ELM (PLANER TREE)
(*Planera aquatica* Gmel.)

The water elm or planer tree is found on low wet flood plains of the larger streams of the eastern part of the State where water stands during several months of the year. It forms a small spreading tree with a low broad head 30 to 40 feet in height and with a maximum trunk diameter of 20 inches.

The BARK is light brown or gray, about one-quarter inch thick, and separates into large scales.

WATER ELM—Nearly natural size.

The LEAVES resemble those of the small-leaved elms. They are 2 to 2½ inches long, three-quarters to 1 inch wide on short stalks, dark dull green above and paler on the lower surface with yellowish veins.

The FLOWERS appear with the leaves in March or early April. The small flowers are sometimes normal, and sometimes the male and female flowers are borne separately on the same tree. The FRUIT is a peculiar rounded, shaggy appearing body, about three-eighths of an inch long. It consists of a nut-like center covered with soft and very irregular wing-like outgrowths which extend out on all sides from the center.

The WOOD is light brown, coarse grained and soft, very light in weight, and has a broad zone of nearly white sapwood. It has no economic value.

44

SOUTHERN HACKBERRY (Sugarberry)
(*Celtis laevigata* Koch., *Celtis mississippinsesis* Spach)

The southern hackberry or sugarberry is found in the eastern part of the State. It occurs most abundantly and of greatest size in rich alluvial soil, but thrives however, on various types of soil from the richest to the poorest. It is usually a small or medium sized tree from 30 to 50 feet high

SOUTHERN HACKBERRY
Leaf and Fruit, one-half natural size. Twig, two-thirds natural size.

and 10 to 20 inches in diameter, though it sometimes gets much larger. Its limbs are spreading or pendulous, forming a broad head, and its branchlets are slender and light green, glabrous or pubescent when young, and bright reddish brown during their first winter. In the open, the crown is very symmetrical. It makes an excellent shade tree.

The BARK is pale gray and covered with prominent excrescences.

The LEAVES are simple, oblong-lanceolate, one-sided, 2½ to 5 inches long, thin, with the edges smooth.

The FLOWERS are not conspicuous, and are borne on slender smooth stems, appearing in April or May, and are of a creamy-greenish color. The FRUIT is short-oblong to pear-shaped, orange-red or yellow, one-fourth inch in diameter, and ripens in September. The sweet character of the fruit has given rise to the name sugarberry, and makes it sought as food by birds and animals.

The WOOD is soft, weak, close-grained, and light yellow, and is used occasionally for flooring and furniture, but chiefly for fuel.

Celtis laevigata var. **texana** is found in western Oklahoma. The leaves are shorter and broader.

45

ROUGH-LEAVED HACKBERRY

(Celtis crassifolia Lam., *C. occidentalis* var. *crassifolia* Gray.)

The rough-leaved hackberry is found in the eastern and in the northwestern parts of the State on various types of soil. It is usually a medium sized to large tree, becoming 60 to 100 feet or more high and 10 to 20 inches in diameter. Its limbs are often crooked and

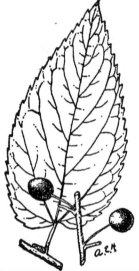

ROUGH-LEAVED HACKBERRY
Leaf, one-third natural size.
Twig, one-half natural size.

angular and bear a head made of slender, pendant branches or short, bristly, stubby twigs. In the open, the crown is generally very symmetrical. It makes an excellent shade tree.

The B A R K is brownish gray, 1 inch or more thick, and generally very rough with many scale-like or warty projections of dead bark.

The LEAVES are simple, ovate, alternate, one-sided, 2 to 4 inches long, thick and very rough a b o v e, green on both surfaces, the edges toothed toward the long point. The FLOWERS are inconspicuous, and the two kinds are borne on the same tree. They appear in April or May, and are of a creamy greenish color. The FRUIT is a round, somewhat oblong drupe or berry, dark purple, one-third of an inch in diameter, ripening in September. It has a thin, purplish skin, and sweet yellowish flesh. The berries frequently hang on the tree most of the winter.

The WOOD is heavy, rather soft, weak, and decays readily when exposed. It is used chiefly for fuel, but occasionally for lumber.

The dog hackberry (*Celtis canina* Raf.) has the more pointed leaves which are thinner and nearly smooth on the upper surface. It also forms a large tree and is occasionally found in this State.

46

RED MULBERRY (*Morus rubra* L.)

The red mulberry occurs in the eastern half of the State. It prefers the rich soils of the lower and middle districts, but is nowhere abundant. It is commonly called mulberry as there are no other native species. The white mulberry and paper mulberry, which are sometimes found in waste places, are introduced species which have to some extent become naturalized.

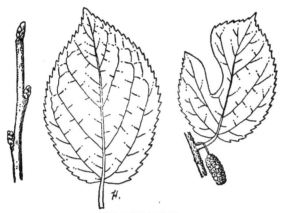

RED MULBERRY

Twig, two-thirds natural size.   Leaf, one-third natural size.

The red mulberry is a small tree, rarely 50 feet high and 2 feet in diameter, often growing in the shade of larger trees.

The BARK is rather thin, dark grayish brown, peeling off in long narrow flakes.

The LEAVES are alternate, thin, rounded or somewhat heart-shaped, toothed, pointed, 3 to 5 inches long, rough hairy above and soft hairy beneath. Often some of the leaves, especially on young trees and thrifty shoots, are mitten-shaped or variously lobed.

The FLOWERS are of two kinds, on the same or different trees, in long drooping catkins, the female catkins shorter, appearing with the leaves. The FRUIT is dark red or black, and resembles a blackberry; however, a stalk extends through it centrally, and it is longer and narrower. The fruit is sweet and edible and greatly relished by birds and various animals.

The WOOD is rather light, soft, not strong, light orange-yellow, very durable in contact with the soil. It is chiefly used for fence posts. The tree might be planted for this purpose and to furnish food for birds.

OSAGE ORANGE (Bois d'Arc)
(*Maclura pomifera* Schm.)

The osage orange, "bowdarc," hedge apple, or mock orange, is found in the valley of the Red River in the southern part of the State. It has been planted considerably as a hedge fence. Occasionally it reaches a height of 60 feet and a diameter of 30 inches, but more usually it is found from 20 to 40 feet in height and from 4 to 12 inches in diameter. This tree is sometimes used for shade, but mostly for hedges and

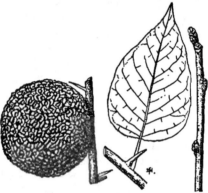

OSAGE ORANGE
Leaf and Fruit, one-quarter natural size.   Twig, two-thirds natural size.

as living fence posts. The BARK is thin, gray, sometimes tinged with yellow, and on old trees divided into strips or flakes. It contains tannin and has been used for tanning leather.

The LEAVES are simple, alternate, oval-pointed and lustrous green on the upper surface, 3 to 5 inches long and 2 to 3 inches wide, and turn bright yellow in the autumn.

The yellowish FLOWERS appear in May. They are of two kinds on the same tree—the male flowers in a linear cluster and the female flowers a rounded ball. The FRUIT is globular, from 2 to 5 inches in diameter, somewhat resembling a very rough green orange.

The WOOD is heavy, exceedingly hard, very strong, and very durable in contact with the soil. The heartwood is bright orange in color, turning brown upon exposure. It is largely used for posts; sometimes for wheel-stock, lumber and fuel. The Indians prized the wood for bows and war clubs.

CUCUMBER TREE (*Magnolia acuminata* L.)

The cucumber tree attains an average height of 40 to 80 feet and a diameter of 1 to 2 feet. It occurs singly among other hardwood trees on the cooler north slopes and coves of Rich Mountain in southeastern Oklahoma.

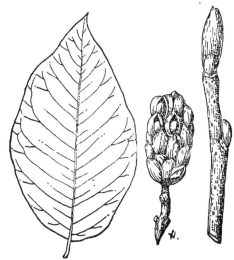

CUCUMBER TREE
Leaf, one-third natural size.
Twig, two-thirds natural size.

The BARK is aromatic and bitter; that of the young twigs is a lustrous red-brown, while the bark of the trunk is rather thin, dark brown, furrowed and broken into thin scales.

The LEAVES are alternate, oblong, short-pointed, rounded at the base, silky hairy when unfolding, later smooth or slightly silky, 6 to 10 inches long, 4 to 6 inches wide, often with wavy edges, dark green above, lighter beneath.

The FLOWERS are single, large—though smaller than those of the other magnolias—2½ to 3 inches long. The six upright petals are whitish green tinged with yellow. The FRUIT is a smooth, dark-red, often crooked "cone," 2½ to 3 inches long, somewhat resembling, when green, a small cucumber. The seeds are one-half inch long, and covered with a pulpy scarlet coat, which attracts the birds, particularly as the seeds hang by thin cords from the opening "cones."

The WOOD is light, soft, close-grained, durable, of a light yellow-brown color. It is quite desirable for ornamental planting. The evergreen **Magnolia grandiflora** L. is frequently cultivated but is probably not native.

49

UMBRELLA TREE (*Magnolia tripetala* L.)

The umbrella tree, sometimes called elkwood, is occasionally found in the southeastern part of the State but is nowhere very common. It occurs along mountain streams in very rich, moist soil and along the margin of swamps. Its name comes from the clusters of very large leaves surrounding the ends of the branchlets remotely resembling an umbrella. It is a small-sized tree usually not exceeding 30 to 35 feet in height with a straight or often inclined trunk up to a foot or more in diameter.

UMBRELLA TREE
Leaf, one-sixth natural size.
Twig, three-fourths natural size.

The BARK is thin, light gray, smooth, and roughened by irregular protruding portions.

The LEAVES vary from 14 to 22 inches long by 8 to 10 inches wide and are borne on stout stems. They are alternate, simple, narrowly pear-shaped or ovate, pointed at both ends, smooth, and fall in the autumn with little change in color. The FLOWERS are creamy white, ill-scented, cup-shaped, with petals 6 to 9 inches long and mostly standing erect, appearing in May. A whorl of leaves usually surrounds the flower. The FRUIT is rose colored when ripe, from 2 to 4 inches long, cylindrical or cone-shaped, consisting of small capsules each containing a red seed about one-half inch in length.

The WOOD is light, soft, close-grained, light brown in color, and without special uses.

The umbrella tree is considerably planted for ornamental purposes both in this country and in parts of Europe.

PAWPAW

(*Asimina triloba* Dunal.)

The pawpaw, which grows as a small tree or large shrub, is found in the eastern part of the State. Most commonly it occurs as an undergrowth in the shade of larger trees, on limestone or very rich alluvial soils. When growing alone, however, it forms a pyramid-

PAPAW

Leaf, one-quarter natural size. Twig, two-thirds natural size.

shaped top. The BARK is thin, dark grayish brown, and smooth, or slightly fissured on old trees.

The LEAVES are alternate on the stem, pear-shaped, with pointed ends and tapering bases, smooth and light green above, from 8 to 10 inches long, and clustered toward the ends of the branches.

The dark-purple, attractive FLOWERS appear with the leaves singly or in twos along the branch, measure nearly 2 inches across, and produce nectar which attracts the bees.

When thoroughly ripe, the FRUIT is delicious and nutritious. It measures from 3 to 5 inches in length, turns from greenish yellow to very dark brown in color, and holds rounded or elongated seeds which separate readily from the pulp.

The WOOD is light, soft or spongy, and weak, greenish to yellow in color, and of no commercial importance.

Because of its handsome foliage, attractive flowers and curious fruit, the pawpaw has been much used in ornamental planting.

51

SASSAFRAS
(*Sassafras officinale* N. and E.)

The sassafras is a small, aromatic tree, usually not over 40 feet in height or a foot in diameter. It is found in the eastern part of the State on dry soils, and is one of the first broad-leaf trees to come up on abandoned fields, where the seeds are dropped by birds. It is closely related to the camphor tree of Japan. The

SASSAFRAS
Twig, one-half natural size. Leaf, one-third natural size.

BARK of the trunk is thick, red-brown and deeply furrowed and that of the twigs is bright green.

The LEAVES are very characteristic. It is one of the few trees having leaves of widely different shape on the same tree, or even on the same twig. Some are oval and entire, 4 to 6 inches long; others have one lobe, resembling the thumb on a mitten; while still others are divided at the outer end into three distinct lobes. The young leaves and twigs are quite mucilaginous.

The FLOWERS are clustered, greenish yellow, and open with the first unfolding of the leaves. The male and female flowers are usually on different trees. The FRUIT is an oblong, dark blue or black, lustrous berry, containing one seed and surrounded at the base by what appears to be a small orange-red or scarlet cup at the end of a scarlet stalk.

The WOOD is light, soft, weak, brittle, and durable in the soil; the heartwood is dull orange-brown. It is used for posts, rails, boat-building, cooperage and for ox-yokes. The bark of the roots yields the very aromatic oil of sassafras much used for flavoring candies and various commercial products.

SWEET GUM (Red Gum)
(*Liquidambar styraciflua* L.)

The sweet gum is a large valuable forest tree. It occurs on rich river bottoms and in swamps subject to frequent overflow, as well as on drier uplands along streams in the eastern part of the State. It is usually abundant in second growth on old fields and in cut-over woods. The BARK is a light gray, roughened by corky scales, later becoming deeply furrowed. After the second year the twigs often develop 2 to 4 corky projections of the bark, which give them a winged appearance. The simple, alternate star-shaped LEAF, with its 5 to 7 points or lobes, is 5 to 7 inches across and very aromatic. In the fall its coloring is brilliant, ranging from pale yellow through orange and red to a deep bronze.

The FLOWERS are of two kinds on the same tree, unfolding with the leaves. The FRUIT at first glance re-

SWEETGUM
Leaf, one-third natural size.
Twig, two-thirds natural size.

minds one of the balls of the sycamore, but on closer inspection proves to be a head. It measures an inch or more in diameter and is made up of many capsules with projecting spines. It frequently hangs on the tree by its long swinging stem late into the winter.

The WOOD is heavy, moderately hard, close-grained, and not durable on exposure. The reddish brown heartwood, which suggests the name red gum, is not present to any appreciable extent in logs under 16 inches in diameter. The wood is extensively used for flooring, interior finish, paper pulp and veneers for baskets of all kinds. Veneers of the heartwoood are largely used in furniture, sometimes as imitation mahogany or circassian walnut.

This tree should be more widely planted for ornamental use.

SYCAMORE
(*Platanus occidentalis* L.)

The sycamore, also called buttonwood, is considered the largest hardwood tree in North America. It occurs in the eastern half of the State and is most abundant and reaches its largest size along streams and on rich bottom lands. It is one of the more rapid-growing trees. It has been successfully planted on sub-irrigated soils in the northwestern part of the State where it has made rapid growth.

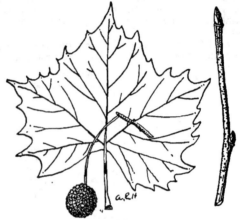

SYCAMORE
Twig, one-half natural size. Leaf and Fruit, one-third natural size.

The BARK of the sycamore is a characteristic feature. On the younger trunk and large limbs it is very smooth, greenish gray in color. The outer bark yearly flakes off in large patches and exposes the nearly white younger bark. Near the base of old trees the bark becomes thick, dark brown and divided by deep furrows.

The LEAVES are simple, alternate, 4 to 7 inches long and about as broad, light green and smooth above, and paler below. The base of the leafstalk is hollow and in falling off exposes the winter bud. The FRUIT is a ball about 1 inch in diameter. conspicuous throughout the winter as it hangs on its flexible stem, which is 3 to 5 inches long During early spring the fruit ball breaks up, and the small seeds are widely scattered by the wind

The WOOD is hard and moderately strong, but decays rapidly in the ground It is used for butchers' blocks, tobacco boxes, furniture and interior finish.

The European sycamore, or planetree, is less subject to disease than our species and has been widely planted in this country for ornament and shade.

SERVICE-BERRY, OR SERVICE-TREE
(*Amelanchier canadensis* Medic.)

The service-tree, also known as service-berry and locally as "sarvis," is found in the northeastern part of the State and attains its best development on the mountain slopes. It is a small tree, 20 to 50 feet high and 6 to 18 inches in diameter, with a rather narrow, rounded top, but is often little more than a shrub. The BARK is thin, ashy gray, smooth on the branches and upper part of the stem, and breaking into shallow fissures on the short trunk.

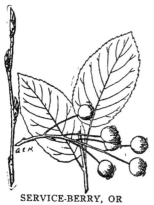

SERVICE-BERRY, OR
SERVICE-TREE
One-half natural size

The LEAVES are alternate, slender - stalked, ovate, pointed, finely toothed, 2 to 4 inches long, purplish brown until nearly mature, then becoming a light green, and early covered with scattered silky hairs.

The white FLOWERS appear in erect or drooping clusters in early spring, before or with the leaves, making the tree quite conspicuous in the leafless or budding forest.

The FRUIT is sweet, edible, rounded, dark purple when ripe, one-third to one-half an inch in diameter, ripening early in June. Birds and other denizens of the forest are very fond of the fruit, and men have been known to cut down and destroy the trees to gather one good crop of fruit.

The WOOD is heavy, exceedingly hard, strong, close-grained and dark brown. It is occasionally used for handles. This is a desirable ornamental tree and should be planted for this purpose and to encourage the birds.

BLACK CHERRY (Wild Cherry)
(*Prunus serotina* Erh.)

A medium-sized tree, up to about 70 feet high and 1 to 3 feet in diameter, black cherry as a tree is at its best in the high mountains. The forest-grown trees have long clear trunks with little taper; open-grown trees have short trunks with many branches and irregular spreading crowns. The BARK on branches and young trunks is smooth and bright reddish brown,

BLACK CHERRY
Twig, two-thirds natural size.   Leaf, one-third natural size.

marked by conspicuous, narrow, white, horizontal lines, and has a bitter-almond taste. On the older trunks the bark becomes rough and broken into thick, irregular plates.

The LEAVES are alternate, simple, oval to lance-like in shape, with edges broken by many fine incurved teeth, thick and shiny above, and paler beneath.

The FRUIT is dull purplish black, about as large as a pea, and is borne in long hanging clusters. It ripens in late summer, and is edible, although it has a slightly bitter taste.

The WOOD is reddish brown with yellowish sapwood, moderately heavy, hard, strong, fine-grained, and does not warp or split in seasoning. It is valuable for its luster and color and is used for furniture, interior finish, tools, and implement handles. With the exception of black walnut, the cherry lumber has a greater unit value than any other hardwood of the eastern United States.

HAWTHORNE (HAW, WHITE HAW, RED HAW, THORN BUSH)
(*Crataegus* species)

The hawthorne, as here treated, represents a considerable number of different species and varieties distributed throughout the eastern half of the State. Members of the group occur on the poorest and richest soils, on the shallowest and deepest, and on the limestone hills as well as on the rich bottom and swamp land. Most of the forms have a common likeness in possessing thorns and bearing white blossoms and red or yellow fruit. Some species are planted as orna-

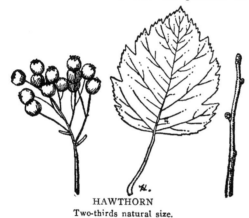

HAWTHORN
Two-thirds natural size.

mental trees, but otherwise the group is of little commercial value.

The BARK is generally thin, gray in color, and on the old stems broken up into thin, narrow scales.

The LEAVES are simple, alternate, mostly oval or wedge-shaped, notched on the edges, and usually from 2 to 3 inches long.

The FLOWERS are white, some fragrant and others with a slightly unpleasant odor; they appear in early spring. The FRUIT varies from globular to oblong, from one-fourth to three-fourths inch in diameter; some when ripe have a pulpy, sweet, edible flesh, surrounding from 1 to 5 bony seeds. The fruit of most species ripens in the fall, and one or two varieties yield a fruit highly prized for making jelly.

The WOOD is strong, tough, heavy, hard, but rarely used for any purpose.

MESQUITE
(*Prosopis juliflora* var. *glandulosa* Cock.)

This well-known small tree of the dry regions of the Southwest is found in the western part of the State. The short trunk, usually only 6 to 8 inches in diameter, divides into many branches forming a loose, open top or crown.

The ROOT system is very large, consisting of a thick taproot sometimes extending downward to a depth of 30 or 40 feet, with many radiating roots spreading horizontally in different directions.

MESQUITE
(*Prosopis juliflora* var. *glandulosa* Cock)

The LEAVES are compound, made up of 12 to 20 leaflets attached along a central midrib, or "stem," from 8 to 10 inches long. The leaflets are smooth, dark green, and pointed, often 2 inches long. **Near** their bases are small spines.

The FLOWERS are tiny and in clusters (spikes) from 2 to 4 inches long. They are fragrant and yield nectar that is sought by the bees. The FRUIT is a pod about 4 to 9 inches and narrowed between each of the 10 to 20 seeds, enclosed in a thick sweet pulp and used by the natives as food. It is also eagerly sought by wild life and livestock.

The WOOD is heavy, hard, and dark reddish brown in color. It is much used for fuel and, because it is very lasting in the ground, for fence posts.

RED BUD (*Cercis canadensis* L.)

The redbud, sometimes called Judas-tree from its oriental relative of that name, is a small tree occurring under taller trees or on the borders of fields on hillsides in valleys throughout the State as far west as Dewey county. It ordinarily attains a height of 25 to 50 feet and a diameter of 6 to 12 inches. Its stout branches usually form a wide flat head.

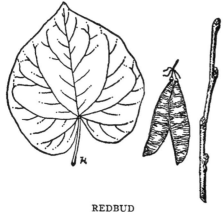

REDBUD
Leaf, one-fifth natural size. Twig, two-thirds natural size.

The BARK is bright red-brown, the long narrow plates separating into thin scales.

The LEAVES are alternate, heart-shaped, entire, 3 to 5 inches long and wide, glossy green turning in autumn to a bright clear yellow.

The conspicuous, bright purplish red, pea-shaped FLOWERS are in numerous clusters along the twigs and small branches and appear before or with the leaves in early spring. With the redbud in its full glory, a drive through the country is likely to be one long remembered.

The FRUIT is an oblong, flattened, many-seeded pod, 2 to 4 inches long, reddish during the summer, and often hanging on the tree most of the winter.

The WOOD is heavy, hard, not strong, rich dark brown in color, and of little commercial importance. The redbud is cultivated as an ornamental tree and for that purpose might be planted more generally in this State.

HONEY LOCUST (*Gleditsia triacanthos* L.)

The honey locust occurs in the eastern and northern parts of the State and has been successfully planted on sub-irrigated soils in the northwestern part. It grows under a wide variety of soil and moisture conditions. It sometimes occurs in the forest, but more commonly in corners and waste places beside roads and fields. It reaches a diameter of 30 inches and a height of 75 feet. The BARK on old trees is dark gray and is divided into thin tight scales. The strong thorns---straight, brown, branched, sharp and shiny which grow on the 1-year-old wood and remain for many years---are sufficient to identify the honey locust.

HONEY LOCUST

Twig, three-quarters natural size.

Leaf, one-quarter natural size.

The LEAF is pinnate or feather-like, with 18 to 28 leaflets; or it is twice-pinnate, consisting of 4 to 7 pairs of pinnate or secondary leaflets, each 6 to 8 inches long and somewhat resembling the leaf of the black locust.

The FRUIT is a pod, 10 to 18 inches long, often twisted, 1 to 1½ inches wide, flat, dark brown or black when ripe and containing yellow sweetish pulp and seeds. The seeds are very hard and each is separated from the others by the pulp. The pods are eaten by many animals, and as the seeds are hard to digest, many are thus widely scattered from the parent tree.

The WOOD is coarse-grained, hard, strong and moderately durable in contact with the ground. It is used for fence posts and crossties. It should not be confused with the very durable wood of the black locust.

BLACK LOCUST (YELLOW LOCUST)
(*Robinia pseudoacacia* L.)

The black locust occurs in the eastern part of 'the State and has been extensively planted nearly all over the State. It is severely attacked by the locust borer which has destroyed large numbers of the trees. The twigs and branchlets are armed with paired straight or slightly curved sharp, strong spines, sometimes as much as 1 inch in length which remain attached to the outer bark for many years. The BARK is dark brown and divides into strips as the tree grows older.

The LEAVES are pinnate, or feather-like, from 6 to 10 inches in length, consisting of from 7 to 19 oblong thin leaflets.

The FLOWERS are fragrant, white or cream-colored, and appear in graceful pendant racemes.

BLACK LOCUST
Leaf and Fruit, one-third natural size.
Twig, two-thirds natural size.

The FRUIT is a pod from 3 to 5 inches long containing 4 to 8 small hard seeds which ripen late in the fall. The pod splits open during the winter, discharging the seeds. Some seeds usually remain attached to each half of the pod, and this acts as a wing upon which the seeds are borne to considerable distance before the strong spring winds.

The WOOD is yellow in color, coarse-grained, very heavy, very hard, strong, and very durable in contact with the soil. It is used extensively for **fence-posts**, poles, tree nails, insulator pins and occasionally for lumber and fuel.

COFFEE TREE (Kentucky Coffee Tree)
Gymnocladus dioicus K. Koch.)

This tree, a member of the pea or bean family (legumes) rises with a straight shaft and, in the open, is topped with a widespreading noticeably light or airy crown made up of graceful foliage evenly distributed. It is found along streams and on low lands throughout the State. Because its seeds in early days were to some extent used as a substitute for coffee, it has become widely known by its present common name.

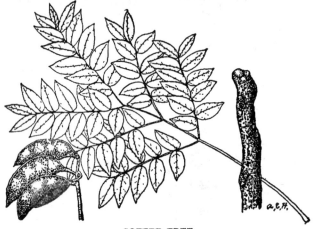

COFFEE TREE
Leaf and Fruit, one-eighth natural size.
Twig, one-half natural size.

The BARK is relatively thin, fissured, dark gray tinged with red, and roughened by numerous small scales.

The LEAVES are alternate, doubly compounded with 5 to 9 pinnae (pairs of leaf branches) each having 6 to 14 smooth leaflets, generally ovate in shape. The complete leaf including the stem measures from 1 to 3 feet in length by 18 to 24 inches in width. The small FLOWERS are borne in clusters, and each individual tree bears only male or female flowers, as the case may be. The FRUIT is a pod, borne several in a cluster. The pods measure from 4 to 10 inches in length, remain closed through the winter, and contain seeds about three-quarters of an inch across, separated by a thick layer of sweet pulp.

The WOOD is heavy, strong, coarse-grained, and durable in contact with the soil. It is occasionally used for cabinet work, and for posts and in general construction.

HOLLY

(Ilex opaca Ait.)

The holly occurs in the southeastern part of the State. It prefers a rich moist soil, but is also found on the higher and drier situations. It is much less abundant now than formerly, due to the large amount gathered and shipped to the cities for Christmas decorations.

It is a small evergreen tree, seldom exceeding 30 feet in height and 12 inches in diameter.

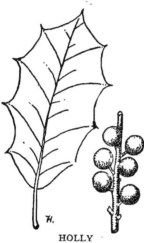

HOLLY
Two-thirds natural size.

The BARK is light gray and roughened by wart-like growths. The numerous short, slender b r a n c h e s form a dense, narrow pyramidal head of s t r i k i n g dark-green color effect, especially when well laden with the conspicuous red berries.

The LEAVES are simple, alternate, oval, thick and leathery, 2 to 4 inches long, and armed with spiny teeth; they persist on the branches for about three years, then they drop off in the spring.

The FLOWERS are small, whitish and inconspicuous; the male and female flowers are usually borne on separate trees.

The FRUIT, which ripens late in the fall and persists on the branches over winter is a dull red or sometimes yellow, nearly round berry, about one-quarter of an inch in diameter containing 4 to 6 ribbed nutlets.

The WOOD is light, tough, not strong, and nearly white. It is valued and much used for cabinet work and wood-turning. For this purpose many of the larger, finer trees have been cut and marketed.

PRICKLY ASH (Toothache Tree)
(*Xanthoxylum clava-herculis* L.)

The prickly ash, or toothache tree, is restricted to the lowlands of the eastern part of the State. It is a very spiny round-headed tree or shrub, becoming 30 feet high or more, with a short trunk 12 to 16 inches in diameter.

The BARK, which is light gray and very thin, is roughened by corky tubercles surrounding the prickles.

PRICKLY ASH
Leaf, one-third natural size. Fruit and Twig, three-quarters natural size.

The tubercles are sometimes nearly an inch across and rounded at the apex. The bark is gathered for its medicinal qualities, being used for toothache and rheumatism. The twigs are brown-hairy at first, becoming smooth, gray and bearing broad-based prickles over a half inch long.

The LEAVES are compound composed of 7 to 17 leaflets on a prickly leaf-stem. The leaflets are oblique at the base, toothed and pointed, 1 to 2½ inches long, lustrous green above, paler and sometimes hairy below, falling in late winter or spring.

The FLOWERS are of two kinds on different trees, in branched clusters, appearing in spring when the leaves are half grown. The FRUIT is borne in dense nearly globose clusters, ripening in May or June. It is a one-seeded, chestnut-brown capsule one-quarter inch long, with a rough surface. The seeds are black and shining.

The WOOD is of light weight, soft, close-grained and light brown, with yellow sapwood.

SUGAR MAPLE
(Acer saccharum Marsh.)

The sugar maple, often called sugar tree, is found only on the cool slopes, usually in limestone soil in the southeastern and northwestern parts of the State. It has a very symmetrical, dense crown, affording heavy shade. The BARK on young trees is light gray to brown and rather smooth, but as the tree grows older it breaks up into long, i r r e g u l a r plates or scales, which vary from gray to a l m o s t black. The twigs are smooth and reddish - b r o w n, and the w i n t e 1 buds sharp-pointed. The tree attains a height of more than 80 feet and a diameter of 2 feet or m o r e. The sap yields maple sugar and maple syrup.

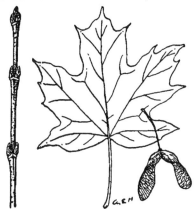

SUGAR MAPLE
Leaf, one-third natural size.
Twig, one-half natural size.

The LEAVES are 3 to 5 inches across, simple, opposite, with 3 to 5 pointed and sparsely toothed lobes, the divisions between the lobes being rounded. The leaves are dark green on the upper surface, lighter green beneath, turning in autumn to brilliant shades ot dark red, scarlet, orange and clear yellow.

The FLOWERS are yellowish green, on long thread-like stalks, appearing with the leaves, the two kinds in separate clusters. The FRUIT, which ripens in the fall, consists of a two-winged "samara," or "key," the two slightly divergent wings about 1 inch in length and containing a seed and carried by the wind.

The WOOD is hard, heavy, strong, close-grained and light brown in color. It is known commercially as hard maple, and is used in the manufacture of flooring, furniture, shoe-lasts and a great variety of novelties.

The variety *grandidentatum* Nutt., is found in the Wichita Mountains in southwestern Oklahoma, but is rare and local.

RED MAPLE (*Acer rubrum* L.)

The red maple, or swamp maple, is found in the eastern and central parts of the State. It is usually a medium-sized tree, quick-growing and relatively short-lived. It is used as a shade tree, though much inferior for this purpose to the other maples, especially the sugar maple. The BARK is smooth and light gray on young stems, and dark gray and rough on the old limbs and trunk.

The LEAVES are 2 to 5 inches long and have from

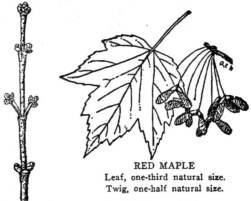

RED MAPLE
Leaf, one-third natural size.
Twig, one-half natural size.

3 to 5 pointed, saw-toothed lobes, which are separated by sharp angular sinuses or openings. The upper surface when mature is light green and the lower surface whitish and partly covered with pale down. In autumn the leaves turn to brilliant shades of red, orange and yellow.

The red FLOWERS in dense clusters appear in early spring before the leaves, the buds turning a deep red sometime before they open. The winter buds are small, red and round or blunt-pointed. The FRUIT ripens in late spring or early summer. It consists of pairs of winged seeds, or keys, one-half to 1 inch in length, on long drooping stems, red, reddish brown or yellow in color.

The WOOD, which is commercially known as soft maple, is heavy, close-grained, rather weak and of a light-brown color. It is used in the manufacture of furniture, and for turnery, woodenware, and also for fuel.

SILVER MAPLE (*Acer saccharinum* L.)

The silver or soft maple occurs rarely except on moist land and along streams in the eastern half of the State. It attains heights of 100 feet or more and diameters of 3 feet or over. It usually has a short trunk which divides into a number of large ascending limbs. These again subdivide, and the small branches droop but turn upward at the tips. The BARK on the old stems is dark gray and broken into long flakes or scales; on the young shoots, it is smooth and varies in color from reddish to a yellowish gray. The silver maple grows rapidly and has been much planted as a shade tree, but is less desirable than many other trees because of its brittleness and suscep-

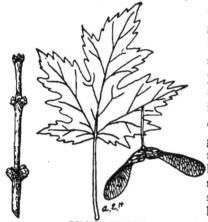

SILVER MAPLE
Twig, one-half natural size.
Leaf, one-third natural size.

tibility to insects and fungus diseases.

The LEAVES are opposite on the stem, have from 3 to 5 lobes ending in long points with toothed edges and are separated by deep angular sinuses or openings; they are pale green on the upper surface and silvery white underneath. The BUDS are rounded, red or reddish brown, blunt-pointed; generally like those of red maple.

The FLOWERS appear in the spring before the leaves, in dense clusters, and are of a greenish yellow color. The FRUIT ripens in late spring. It consists of a pair of winged seeds or "keys" with wings 1 to 2 inches long on slender, flexible, thread-like stems about an inch long.

The WOOD is soft, weak, even-textured, rather brittle, easily worked, and decays readily when exposed. It is occasionally used for flooring, furniture and fuel.

BOX ELDER (*Acer negundo* L.)

The box elder is a fairly rapid-growing tree, found in the eastern and central parts of the State on alluvial soil. It is a tree of medium size, rarely reaching over 24 inches in diameter and 60 to 70 feet in height. It has been considerably planted for shade because in good soil its growth is rapid. Its limbs and branches, however, are fragile, and the tree as a whole is subject to disease and the depredations of insects. It is not long-lived or generally satisfactory for any purpose.

BOX ELDER
Twig, two-thirds natural size. Leaf, one-third natural size.

It is prolific in reproduction but is largely destroyed by grazing and cultivation.

The BARK on young branches is smooth and green in color; on old trees it is thin, grayish to light brown and deeply divided.

The LEAVES are compound, with usually 3 leaflets (rarely 5 to 7), opposite, smooth and lustrous, green and borne on a leaf-stem or petiole 2 to 3 inches long. The leaflets are 2 to 4 inches long by 1 to 2 inches wide, making the whole leaf 5 to 8 inches in length.

The SEED is a samara, or key, winged similarly to that of a sugar maple, but smaller. It ripens in late summer or early fall, and so is like its close relative, the sugar maple, but unlike its other close relatives, the red maple and silver maple.

The WOOD is soft, light, weak, close-grained, and decays readily in contact with heat and moisture. It is used occasionally for fuel.

In the variety **texana** Pax., found in southeastern Oklahoma, a dense covering of pale hairs clothes the branchlets, and early in the season, the midribs of the leaves.

OHIO BUCKEYE (Fetid Buckeye)
(*Aesculus glabra* var. *leucodermis* Sarg.*)

The Ohio buckeye occurs along streams and in rich soil scattered through central and eastern Oklahoma. Though it is often only a shrub it becomes a medium-sized tree in rich alluvial bottoms, but forms no considerable part of the forest stand. Its LEAVES and FRUIT are poisonous to stock. The crown, or head, is generally open and made up of small spreading branches and twigs orange-brown to reddish brown in

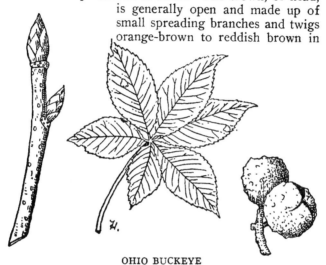

OHIO BUCKEYE
Twig, two-thirds natural size. Nut, one-third natural size.
Leaf, one-quarter natural size.

color. The BARK is light gray and, on old trees, divided or broken into flat scales, which make the stem of the tree rough; the bark is ill-smelling when bruised.

The LEAVES are compound or star-shaped, opposite on the stem, and generally like those of the yellow or sweet buckeye, though smaller and fetid or ill-smelling. They usually turn yellow in the summer and then fall off.

The FLOWERS are cream-colored and appear in clusters, 5 to 8 inches long in April or May. The FRUIT is regularly rounded, pale brown, generally thin-walled, roughened with blunt prickles or warts and, breaking into 2 or 3 valves, discloses the bright, shiny mahogany colored seeds, or nuts.

The WOOD is light, soft and weak, and decays rapidly when exposed. It is used for woodenware, artificial limbs, paper pulp, and for lumber and fuel.

BASSWOOD, OR LINDEN (*Tilia* species)

The lindens, basswoods or lins, are a group of forest trees distinctive, yet as a group so similar that they are being considered together. They grow chiefly in the mountains of the eastern part of the State where they are common and valuable timber trees, attaining heights of 80 feet and diameters of 4 feet. The BARK is light brown, deeply furrowed, and is often peeled for making rough camp buildings. The inner bark furnishes bast for making mats.

LINDEN, OR BASSWOOD
Leaf, one-third natural size.
Twig, one-half natural size.

The LEAVES are more or less heart-shaped, 3 to 6 inches long, thin, saw-toothed, smooth on both sides in some species, but woolly on the under surface of others.

The FLOWERS are yellowish white, in drooping clusters opening in early summer, and the flower-stem is united to the middle of a long, narrow, leaf-like bract. They are very fragrant and from them the bees make large amounts of choice-grade honey.

The FRUIT is a berry-like, dry, 1 to 2 seeded and rounded pod, one-quarter to one-half an inch in diameter, covered with short, thick and brownish wool. It remains attached in clusters to the leafy bract, which later acts as a wing to bear it away on the wind.

The WOOD is light, soft, tough, not durable, light brown in color. It is used in the manufacture of pulp, woodenware, furniture, trunks, excelsior, and many other articles.

DOGWOOD (*Cornus florida* L.)

The dogwood, often referred to as flowering dogwood, is found growing in the eastern half of the State, usually under the larger forest trees. It is a small tree, usually 15 to 30 feet high and 6 to 12 inches in diameter, occasionally larger, with a rather flat and spreading crown and short, often crooked trunk. The BARK is reddish brown to black and broken up into small 4-sided scaly blocks.

DOGWOOD

Leaf, one-half natural size.
Twig, two-thirds natural size.

The LEAVES are opposite, ovate, 3 to 5 inches long, 2 to 3 inches wide, pointed, entire or wavy on the margin, bright green above, pale green or grayish beneath.

The FLOWERS, which unfold from the conspicuous, round, grayish, winter flower buds before the leaves come out, are small, greenish yellow, arranged in dense heads surrounded by large white or rarely pinkish petal-like bracts, which give the appearance of large spreading flowers 2 to 4 inches across.

The FRUIT is a bright scarlet "berry," one-half an inch long and containing a hard nutlet in which are one or two seeds. Usually several fruits, or "berries," are contained in one head. They are relished by birds, squirrels and other animals.

The WOOD is hard, heavy, strong, very close-grained, brown to red in color. It is in great demand for cotton-mill machinery, turnery handles and forms. One other tree has quite similar wood---the persimmon.

The dogwood, with its masses of early spring flowers, its dark-red autumn foliage and its bright-red berries, is probably our most ornamental native tree. It should be used much more extensively in roadside and ornamental planting.

BLACK GUM (*Nyssa sylvatica* March.)

The black gum, often called sour gum, is found in the eastern part of the State. It is considered one of the weed trees of the forest and may be found in many types of soil and conditions of soil moisture. In the lowlands it is occasionally found in year-round swamps with cypress, and in the hills and mountains on dry slopes with oaks and hickories.

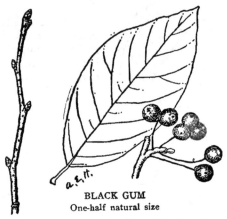

BLACK GUM
One-half natural size

The LEAVES are simple, 2 to 3 inches long, entire, often broader near the apex, shiny, and dark green in color. In the fall the leaves turn a most brilliant red.

The BARK on younger trees is furrowed between flat ridges, and gradually develops into quadrangular blocks that are dense, hard and nearly black.

The greenish FLOWERS on long slender stems appear in early spring when the leaves are about one-third grown. They are usually of two kinds, the male in many-flowered heads and the female in two to several-flowered clusters on different trees. The FRUIT is a dark blue, fleshy berry, two-thirds of an inch long, containing a single hard-shelled seed, and is borne on long stems, 2 to 3 in a cluster.

The WOOD is very tough, cross-grained, not durable in contact with the soil, hard to work, and warps easily. It is used for crate and basket veneers, box shooks, rollers, mallets, rough floors, mine trams, pulpwood, and fuel. In the old days, the hollow trunks were used for "bee-gums."

PERSIMMON (*Diospyros virginiana* L.)

The persimmon, often called "simmon," is well known throughout its range. It is a small tree, rarely exceeding 50 feet in height and 18 inches in diameter, occurring in the eastern and central parts of the State, except in the high mountains. It seems to prefer dry, open situations, and is most abundant in old fields, though it occurs on rich bottomlands. The BARK of old trees is almost black and separated into thick nearly square blocks, much like the black gum.

The LEAVES are alternate, oval, entire, 4 to 6 inches long, dark green and shining above, paler beneath.

The small FLOWERS, which appear in May, are yellowish or cream-white, somewhat bell-shaped, the two kinds occurring on separate trees; the male in clusters of 2 or 3, the female solitary. They are visited by many insects.

PERSIMMON
Leaf, one-half natural size.
Twig, three-quarters natural size.

The FRUIT is a pulpy, round, orange-colored or brown berry, an inch or more in diameter and containing several flattened, hard, smooth seeds. It is strongly astringent while green, but often quite sweet and delicious when thoroughly ripe. It is much relished by children, and by dogs, 'opossums and other animals.

The WOOD is hard, dense, heavy, strong, the heartwood brown or black, the wide sapwood white or yellowish. It is particularly valued for shuttles, golf-stick heads, and similar special uses, but is not of sufficient commercial use to warrant its general encouragement as a timber tree.

WOOLLY BUCKTHORN
(*Bumelia languinosa* Michx.)

The woolly buckthorn is also called chittimwood or gum elastic and grows in sandy woods and thickets. It is found in the eastern part of the State and as far west as Roger Mills county. Though it becomes a medium-sized tree up to 30 feet high with a tall straight trunk over a foot in diameter, it is usually much smaller or even shrubby. Its branches are short,

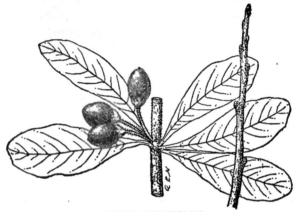

WOOLLY BUCKTHORN
Three-quarters natural size.

straight, and stiff. The twigs are covered with thick biown wood at first, but becomes nearly smooth, reddish brown to ashy gray.

The BARK is up to one-half inch thick, gray on younger branches, becoming brownish gray, broken up into narrow ridges of thick appressed scales.

The LEAVES are 1½ to 2½ inches long, narrow, obovate, rounded at the apex and gradually narrowed toward the base. They are coated when they unfold with a rusty long tomentum, become smooth, dark-green and lustrous above, remaining coated with long, sometimes silvery white, hairs below. The leaves are often clustered in short spurs, subtending clusters of the small flowers or fruits. The twigs may or may not be spiny.

The FLOWERS are small, perfect with 5 petals and 5 sepals (each set united into a cup), 5 stamens, and a single pistil which later forms a black fruit, one-half inch long, fleshy and drupe-like, or berry-like.

The WOOD is heavy but weak, close-grained, light brown streaked with white. The sapwood is yellowish. The woolly buckthorn furnishes a clear viscid "gum elastic" from freshly cut stem wounds.

SWAMP PRIVET
(*Forestiera acuminata* Michx.)

The forestiera or swamp privet is found along river banks, along lakes and standing water in the low land sections of eastern Oklahoma. It is usually a large shrub but often becomes a small tree, less than 30 or 40 feet high, with a short trunk usually less than 3 inches in diameter. Its youngest branches are slender, somewhat hairy, slightly angular, and vary in color from yellowish-green to brown. They become darker and more rounded the second season.

SWAMP PRIVET
Two-thirds natural size.

The BARK is thin, dark brown to brownish-gray, close and slightly ridged.

The LEAVES are opposite, 2½ to 4 inches long, 1 to 1½ inches wide, petioled, and long pointed at both ends, yellowish-green on the upper surface, paler on the lower and slightly toothed above the middle.

The FLOWERS appear in April before the leaves. They are of two kinds, borne separately on the same tree, rather small and in clusters.

The FRUIT falls as soon as ripe in May or June. It is oblong in shape, covered with a tough dry pulp, slightly curved when young (about an inch long and one-quarter inch wide), and tipped with a point. It is deep purple and contains a one-seeded stone.

The WOOD is close-grained, yellowish brown, weak and rather soft. It has no economic use.

75

WHITE ASH (*Fraxinus americana* L.)

The white ash is found in the northern and eastern parts of the State, but grows to best advantage in the rich moist soils of the mountains and river bottom lands. The BARK varies in color from a light gray and a dark brown. The rather narrow ridges are separated with marked regularity by deep, diamond-shaped fissures.

The LEAVES of the white ash are from 8 to 12 inches long and have from 5 to 9 plainly stalked, sharp-

WHITE ASH
Twig, one-half natural size. Leaf, one-third natural size.

pointed leaflets, dark green and smooth above, pale green beneath. The ashes form the only group of trees in eastern America that have opposite, compound leaves with 5 or more leaflets. This fact in itself provides a ready means of identifying the group. The FLOWERS are of two kinds on different trees, the male in dense reddish purple clusters and the female in more open bunches. The FRUIT of the ash is winged, 1 to 1½ inches long, resembling the blade of a canoe paddle in outline, with the seed at the handle end. The fruits mature in late summer and are distributed effectively by the winds.

The WOOD of the white ash is extremely valuable on account of its toughness and elasticity. It is preferred to all other native woods for small tool handles, such athletic implements as rackets, bats and oars, and agricultural implements. It is also used extensively for furniture and interior finish.

BLUE ASH
(*Fraxinus quadrangulata* Michx.)

The blue ash is not very common but is found in the upland portions of the northeastern part of the State, where it is limited to limestone bluffs, occasionally descending to the adjacent bottom lands. It becomes a large tree 60 feet or more in height with a trunk 2 feet in diameter. The young twigs afford the most characteristic feature of this species as they are usu-

BLUE ASH
Leaf, one-third natural size.
Fruit and Twig, two-thirds natural size.

ally square, sometimes winged or 4-ridged between the leaf bases.

The BARK is light gray tinged with red, one-half to two-thirds inch thick, irregularly divided into large plate-like scales. Macerating the inner bark in water yields a blue dye.

The LEAVES are opposite, compound, 8 to 12 inches long, having 7 to 11 stalked leaflets, long pointed and coarsely toothed. The leaves are thick and firm, smooth and yellowish-green above, paler beneath.

The FLOWERS are without petals and appear in clusters when the buds begin to expand.

The FRUIT is flattened and oblong, 1 to 2 inches long and less than a half inch wide and usually notched at the outer end. The wing is about twice the length of the seed-bearing portion and extends down the sides past the middle.

The WOOD is heavy, hard, and close-grained, light yellow, streaked with brown, with a very broad zone of lighter sapwood It is used for flooring and wagon making, and is not usually distinguished commercially from the wood of other ashes.

GREEN ASH (River Ash)
(*Fraxinus pennsylvanica lancelata* (Bork.) Sarg.)

The green ash is a common tree, most abundant in valleys along streams. The hairy form of this tree is known as the red ash. It is found throughout the State as far west as Comanche county and attains a height of 50 feet or more, has spreading branches and a trunk ranging up to 2 feet in diameter. The twigs are smooth, round, and ashy gray marked by pale lenticels and rusty bud-scales.

GREEN ASH
Fruit, two-thirds natural size.
Leaf, one-third natural size.
Twig, three-quarters natural size.

The BARK is a half inch thick or more, brown, tinged with red and slightly furrowed or ridged. The LEAVES are attached opposite on the stem, compound, 10 to 12 inches long, 7 to 9 stalked leaflets which are pointed and slightly toothed on the margin. This species differs from the white ash in having the leaves bright green or yellow-green on both sides.

The FLOWERS are small, the male and female flowers occurring on different trees.

The FRUIT is flat and winged, 1 to 2½ inches long and one-quarter to one-third inch wide, with the wing portion extending well down past the middle of the seed-bearing part, and with the wing sometimes square or slightly notched at the outer end.

The WOOD is heavy, hard, rather strong, brittle and coarse-grained, light brown, with a rather broad layer of light sapwood. It is valuable and used for the same purposes, though not as desirable, as the white ash.

CATALPA (*Catalpa speciosa* Engelm.)

This tree, often miscalled "catawba," is native to the central Mississippi River basin, but has been widely planted and has spread somewhat farther as a result of cultivation. It is found sparsely throughout the State except in the mountains, and occurs on various qualities of soil, but most frequently on rich, moist soil, such as bottoms. It is a medium-sized tree, usually not exceeding 40 to 50 feet in height and 12 to 15 inches in diameter. The trunk is usually short and the head broad with spreading branches. The BARK varies from dark gray to brown, slightly rough, being divided into narrow strips or flakes. Because of its attractive flowers and conspicuous heart-shaped leaves, it is considerably used for shade and ornament.

CATALPA
Leaf, one-third natural size.
Twig, two-thirds natural size.

The LEAVES are simple, opposite, oval, long-pointed, 6 to 10 inches long, and heart-shaped at the base. The catalpa Sphinx moth is a pest and sometimes defoliates the tree.

The FLOWERS appear in clusters or panicles in May or June. They are white with purple and yellow markings, and this makes them decidedly showy and attractive. The FRUIT consists of a bean-like pod, 8 to 16 inches long and from three-eighths to one-half inch in diameter. It hangs on the tree over winter and gradually splits into 2 parts, or valves. The seeds are about 1 inch long and terminate in wings that are rounded and short-fringed at the ends. They are freely carried by the wind.

The WOOD is rather soft, light, coarse-grained, and durable in contact with the soil. It is used for fence posts, poles and fuel, and occasionally for railroad ties. It is a mistake to attempt to grow catalpa for fence posts or other uses except on good agricultural soil.

SOUTHERN BLACK HAW
(*Viburnum rufidulum* Raf.)

The southern black haw is found on hillsides and along the margins of bottom lands in woods and thickets in eastern and southwestern Oklahoma (on the Wichita Mountains). It forms a tree sometimes 35 feet high with a trunk over a foot in diameter but is usually smaller, often flowering as a shrub. The twigs are ashey-gray, becoming dark dull reddish-brown after one to several years. The winter buds are densely covered with rusty brown hairs which persist for some weeks at the base of the leaf-stalks.

The BARK is one-quarter to one - half inch thick becoming roughened into small plate-like dark brown scales tinged with red The bark has medicinal use.

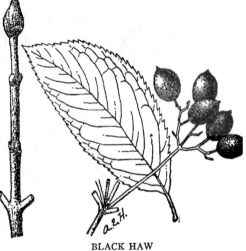

BLACK HAW
Three-quarters natural size.

The LEAVES are attached opposite each other on the stem, elliptic to obovate or oval, pointed or blunt at the apex, wedge-shaped or rounded at the base, and with fine teeth on the margin. They are leathery in texture, very shining and dark green above, pale and dull below, about 3 inches long and 1 to 1½ inches wide.

The FLOWERS are small and white, and each has five petals and five stamens, appearing in the spring, in dense clusters at the tips of branches.

The FRUIT is also clustered, and ripens in October. It is a bright-blue oval drupe or berry, over one-half inch long, covered with a glaucous bloom, and containing a stony seed one-half inch long and one-third inch wide.

The WOOD is bad smelling and has no economic use. The tree is occasionally cultivated and is desirable for decorative planting.

CPSIA information can be obtained
at www.ICGtesting.com
Printed in the USA
BVHW041646081221
623539BV00010B/901

9 781258 467302